Good Growth

Business has a sustainability problem—and sustainability has a business problem, as many companies are fearful of engaging with social and environmental issues, owing to the costs and risks.

Addressing these dual challenges head on, this book provides a blueprint for putting social and environmental benefits at the center of a company's growth agenda. Many sustainability books offer 30,000-foot strategic views and broad-brush guidance on the business of "doing well by doing good," but here is a ground-level guide for profitably integrating social and environmental benefits into individual products and brands. The book introduces the rapidly emerging phenomenon of social impact markets and shows how companies can capitalize on these new pockets of consumer demand through focused strategy, data-informed implementation, and a clear eye on the future, including how digital technologies are creating new ways for brands to expand their social impact and make social mission a central element of competitive strategy.

Weaving together rich case studies and practical tools, this research-backed and real-world-ready guide fills a critical niche: a hands-on strategy playbook for the executives charged with driving brands' top-line growth, making it essential reading for C-suite leaders, R&D, product, and brand managers, board members, NGOs, as well as MBA and executive education students.

Omar Rodríguez Vilá, PhD, is an award-winning marketing professor at Emory University's Goizueta Business School. His research focuses on modern marketing practices and the relationship between social impact and brand growth. He is a frequent speaker at industry conferences and a former global marketing executive at The Coca-Cola Company. Dr. Rodríguez Vilá earned a PhD in Marketing from Emory University and an MBA from Northwestern University. He lives in Atlanta with his daughters Shanti and Lucca.

Sundar Bharadwaj, PhD, is the Coca-Cola Company Chair Professor of Marketing at the Terry College of Business, University of Georgia. He has held tenured or visiting faculty positions at Emory University, the Wharton School, the Indian School of Business, HEC (Paris), Singapore Management University, and BI (Oslo). His research focuses on financial market outcomes and the societal impact of marketing. He has held brand management and sales management positions at several multinational firms.

Good Growth

How Brands Win with Social Impact

Omar Rodríguez Vilá and Sundar Bharadwaj

Routledge
Taylor & Francis Group

NEW YORK AND LONDON

Designed cover image: Getty Images

First published 2025
by Routledge
605 Third Avenue, New York, NY 10158

and by Routledge
4 Park Square, Milton Park, Abingdon, Oxon OX14 4RN

Routledge is an imprint of the Taylor & Francis Group, an informa business

ISBN: 978-1-032-46780-1 (hbk)
ISBN: 978-1-032-46779-5 (pbk)
ISBN: 978-1-003-38324-6 (ebk)

DOI: 10.4324/9781003383246

Typeset in Sabon
by Taylor & Francis Books

"A Shanti y Lucca – por la inspiración y orgullo que brindan a mi vida."
Omar Rodríguez Vilá

"To Anandhi, Shashank, and Abinav for their constant
encouragement and healthy skepticism."
Sundar Bharadwaj

Contents

Figures

Acknowledgments

This book is the result of many years of work that included research projects, conversations with students, engagements with clients, and dozens of hours of teaching. Therefore, the ideas presented here have been influenced by many people, not all of whom we are able to mention by name. But below are some of the people that were most instrumental to our thinking. We would like to start by thanking the Business and Society Institute at Emory University and its director, Dr. Wesley Longhofer, as well as the Ray C. Anderson Center for Sustainable Business at Georgia Tech and its director, Dr. Beril Toktay. Both supported our research through funding and exposure. Dr. Toktay was instrumental in creating many teaching opportunities for the material. Early partners in our efforts also include Sustainable Brands and its founder KoAnn Vikoren Skrzyniarz, who helped us get access to many of the Chief Sustainability Officers and Chief Marketing Officers that participated in our different studies. Sheryl Daija, executive director of BRIDGE—was instrumental in our study of inclusion in business. The MMA—another leading marketing industry trade group—and its CEO Greg Stuart also provided funding and opportunities for some of our research across industries. Important individual contributors to our work include Ricardo Caceres, who helped champion the work and created opportunities for us to apply the ideas and concepts across different companies. C. B. Bhattacharya, a leading scholar in issues of sustainability and marketing, also collaborated with us in the early days of our work, and we are grateful for his support and contribution. We are also grateful to Dr. Robert Kazanjian and his contributions to the SunTrust case. We want to thank the colleagues, managers, and friends who took time to review areas of our work and provide us valuable suggestions: particularly Dr. Ryan Hamilton and Dr. Rajan Varadarajan for their thoughtful and thorough feedback. We would also like to thank Andres Kiger, Peter Schelstraete, Martha Rodriguez, Andrew Hollister, and Alpa Sutaria for their valuable comments, suggestions, and examples. Thank you to all our students who through their questions and discussions during class helped bring practicality and meaning to the work. In particular, thank you to Mehreen Azam for all her help in the final editing stages of the book. Lastly, we want to express our immense gratitude to Dr. Mary Jo Lechowicz, Joel Andrews, and all the staff of nurses, administrators, and doctors at the Winship Cancer Institute of Emory University. Without them, one of us would not have been able to finish this work.

Introduction

Growth is a fundamental goal of most businesses. Growth in sales, growth in profits, growth in customers. The value of companies and the career prospects of their leaders are tied to growth in its many forms. But is all growth…"good growth"? Is there such a thing as "bad growth"? Does the difference matter? In this book, we argue that yes, there is a difference, and yes, it matters. Importantly, no manager is, in fact, working to achieve "bad growth." "Bad growth" is a consequence, not a goal. It is the result of managers trained and incentivized to focus solely on the short-term results the financial community needs, without accounting for social or environmental costs that eventually threaten the sustainability of their business and our planet. In fact, the 20th century was defined by the pursuit of growth without this distinction, leading to many instances of "bad growth." Products that created convenience for consumers but resulted in global pollution of our planet. Economic activity lifted many out of poverty but exhausted natural resources. Energy solutions democratized access to electricity and mobility but now threaten our climate. Some argue the problem is growth itself, that growth is not possible without destruction, that growth is, by its very nature, not sustainable.

We propose a different perspective—that growth is essential for prosperity. The innovation and imagination stimulated by the battle for growth between companies, brands, and leaders are the ingredients needed to resolve the problems of the past and find a new equilibrium between our economy and ecology. We need a new type of growth where social impact is central to the ability of products and services to win in the marketplace—a type of growth we call "good growth." This book offers a blueprint for how to create it by bringing together work from different sources, including academic research, industry studies, direct project experiences, and dozens of interviews with pioneering business leaders that, through their actions, are collectively inventing the "good growth" way.

However, it is important to recognize that "good growth" is not what most marketing managers and business leaders are thinking about today. Their attention is consumed by trying to figure out how to leverage new

DOI: 10.4324/9781003383246-1

data and technologies like GenAI to stay ahead. In fact, the battle for growth has been framed as a technological one. Despite this reality, there is a quiet transformation shaping how new players and historical incumbents compete. Pioneering brand leaders are increasingly finding ways to integrate acts of social impact into the experience of customers, users, or buyers in ways that help them win. Think of On, the Swiss-based company founded by former Swiss Ironman champion Olivier Bernhard with David Allemann and Caspar Coppetti. Their introduction of the Cloudboom Strike LS distance running shoe is changing the game[1]. Described by some as the Tesla of the sneaker world because of its potential for disruption—not only for its 6-ounce weight or its proven strength after Kenyan distance runner Hellen Obiri wore it during her Boston Marathon win, but also because of the way it is produced. Running shoes usually take between 150 to 200 components to make. The Cloudboom Strike LS requires only seven. Every aspect of the shoe production has been reimagined—significantly reducing time, cost, material, waste, and energy requirements. In fact, their environmental footprint is 75 percent less than regular sneakers. Some believe their innovation may not only alter styles, but also change the business model of the industry itself. But what is their edge? Is it performance? Is it style? Is it comfort? Is it environmental impact? It's all of those, and, importantly, the social impact is blended into their value proposition, not tagged along as a promotional conditional on your purchase.

The idea of competing on social impact is far from new. Yet, historically, marketers have associated it with support for a cause through tactical and short-lived efforts. Today, more brand leaders are creating "good growth" by strategically weaving social impact into how they compete for our attention, consideration, and choice. This book is about capturing the lessons from their efforts and helping new leaders create "good growth."

It is important to clarify terms, particularly in this area which has been inundated by varying descriptions. For us, social impact refers to the significant, positive change to communities or the environment resulting from a brand or business's actions. It encompasses improvements in social well-being, environmental sustainability, economic development, and quality of life. Acts of social impact have become embedded into the marketplace in many ways. Electric vehicles, support for Women and Black entrepreneurs, inclusive lines of makeup, paper straws, alternatives to plastic bags, clothes washed with cold water, non-alcoholic beer, technology designed for people with disabilities, and many more. A study of the effect of social impact on the growth of packaged-goods products by IRi and New York University finds that offerings with social impact grew 1.5 times more rapidly than those without. Importantly, while they captured 18 percent of the market, their sales performance represented 30 percent of the growth since 2013[2]. Embedding a social impact benefit has become common in many startups over the past decade. Warby Parker, Toms, Blueland, Bevi, Boxed Water,

Allbirds, and On are just a few of the hundreds of new businesses started since 2010 with a societal benefit central to their offering. For instance, Nimble, started in 2018 by Ross Howe, Jon Bradley, and Kevin Malinowski, is a Certified B Corporation that uses recycled plastics, organic hemp, and aluminum in its products. They also offer free e-waste recycling with every product purchase and facilitate product repairs instead of promoting the purchase of new ones. Like Nimble, there are more than 7,000 certified B Corporations that adopt sustainability principles across most areas of their business operations. The financial community has also embraced the role of social impact, using Environmental, Social, and Governance (ESG) ratings as a part of the standard criteria for evaluating firm risk and growth prospects. Regulatory changes, particularly in Europe and parts of Asia, North America, and South America, are also creating new requirements and incentives for businesses to generate or adopt more sustainable practices. Business schools have significantly increased the offering of programs and courses, focusing on social impact, climate change, and the design of more sustainable business models and solutions. The Business & Society Institute at Emory University and the Ray C. Anderson Center for Sustainable Business at Georgia Tech are two of the many programs dedicated to integrating social impact and sustainability education in business.

Despite the actions of entrepreneurs, investors, and universities, social impact has yet to fully capture the attention of senior leaders and managers at many companies. It is common for issues of sustainability to be framed as risk management or corporate social responsibility commitments instead of strategically critical investments targeted at opportunities to help a brand or company win in the market. The annual report on the state of marketing by Duke University and Deloitte Consulting reported in 2024 that marketing investments related to sustainability represented approximately 1.9 percent of the budget. In the same study, the most adopted action taken by marketing teams to address climate change was recycling, which was adopted by only 37 percent of firms. Building more sustainable products or embedding social impact in the organization were ranked lowest in terms of priority for marketers. Instead, most of the attention in marketing conferences and articles is diverted to developing and adopting new marketing technology tools—in particular, the potential of Artificial Intelligence to transform the discipline. There is little doubt about the importance of technology in optimizing marketing investments today, but the environmental and social challenges facing many industries and brands have a similar transformative power. The societal impact of a product or service can become a driver of growth and disruption, providing brands with a lasting advantage. This book is about how to turn that promise into reality.

Our book covers three basic areas that we believe can unlock the potential for "good growth." First, is the way we think about social impact. We propose a shift in how leaders frequently understand sustainability issues, which is to consider them not as a company's responsibility but as a market. A market forms when a large enough group of people make purchase decisions based on certain features or benefits. In the same way, a growing number of people and businesses are making purchase decisions influenced by the offering's social impact. Be it energy conservation, plastic waste and carbon emissions reduction, or greater inclusion practices, these actions have become features that can not only differentiate a brand but also help it win. We discuss the factors giving rise to social impact markets, how they vary by industry and product category, and, most importantly, how managers can measure and establish the size of the social impact market in their industry. Understanding the social impact market is crucial. It will create the motivation and impetus to shift social impact work out of the corporate responsibility conversation and into the growth strategy conversation.

Second, we outline how to craft a social impact strategy, deciding which societal need to focus on and what role to play as a brand or company. Through discussion and case studies, the book describes a playbook that guides these choices regardless of industry. Finally, competing on social impact is neither an entirely new endeavor, nor is it business as usual. Our research into dozens of companies and leaders on the edge of this work has uncovered a set of practices unique to building social impact capabilities. In the latter part of the book, we outline marketing practices, measurement practices, and leadership practices that can help any manager turn the ideas presented here into action. We hope that the stories, examples, and methods proposed in this book inspire a new way of thinking about the relationship between profit and social impact, enabling practices that can advance your position in the market and your contribution to society.

Notes

1 *The New York Times* (2024). "On Running Shoes Cloudboom Strike LS Spray-On." *The New York Times*, July 15. Retrieved October 13, 2024.
2 NYU Stern Center for Sustainable Business (n.d.). *Sustainable Market Share Index*[TM]. New York: NYU Stern Center for Sustainable Business.

Chapter 1

The Rise of Social Impact Markets

When does a company grow? When it has access to capital? When it has experienced or effective management? When market conditions play to its favor? When it has the right capabilities? All these factors play critical roles in driving growth. However, it is hard for a company to grow over time in a competitive environment if it does not find customers. Customers are created when managers or entrepreneurs develop offerings that serve the market's needs better than their competitors. Interestingly, creating new product categories has historically been associated with a societal benefit. For instance, home versions of washing machines, introduced in the 1930s, brought much-needed convenience to people and had unintended benefits. The presence of washing machines and other durable goods like refrigerators, vacuum cleaners, and electric stoves saved the time and effort needed to complete household chores and enabled greater participation of women in the workplace[1]. Bar soap is an ancient solution to clean our bodies. Still, the advent of bar soap specifically designed to kill bacteria was an essential public health innovation to slow the rate of a pandemic and limit infections[2]. Brands like Lifebuoy have grown in a platform of personal and societal benefits for years, seeking to expand hand-washing habits and reduce the incidence of waterborne illnesses such as cholera. At the same time, as hand washing habits expand, so does Lifebuoy's business. These examples illustrate one point: products and services that grow often combine positive personal and social impact. However, as companies expand, the pressures to deliver financial outcomes can separate them from the societal benefits they once created. Social effects are relegated as secondary or irrelevant to their ability to compete. In fact, over time, they can begin to see the pursuit or promotion of societal benefits as risky, distracting, or limiting to their economic performance. Their view on growth becomes focused on shareholder value and competitive strategies, prioritizing operating costs or product quality, leaving aside a critical asset—their social impact. The consequences of this separation can be dire, as illustrated in the 2024 Netflix documentary "Buy Now." It offers a grim picture of what happens when the lack of consideration to the "end of life" in products and the single-minded pursuit of more sales result in the accelerating destruction of our planet.

DOI: 10.4324/9781003383246-2

In this book, we present another way of finding growth that blends commercial and societal goals in creating what we call "good growth." The growth results from making personal and social benefits in ways that traditional competition does not. Competing on social impact provides a powerful new dimension for value creation and competitive differentiation that can be layered on top of existing ones, giving brands a decisive edge in a crowded marketplace and enabling more significant levels of meaning and satisfaction for those who lead them. The idea of embedding societal benefits into commercial products is not new. The last two decades have seen many efforts to promote more active participation of the business sector in solving societal problems or needs. The seminal work by Michael Porter on Creating Shared Value, along with the concept of Conscious or Stakeholder Capitalism, the growth of B Corporations, and the adoption of Environmental, Social, and Governance (ESG) ratings and metrics are all indicators of the pursuit of commercial and economic activities that balance investor profitability with the potential of businesses to address critical societal needs. This book is about how to make such integration happen in the relationship with customers by understanding the opportunity to compete on social impact as a new type of capability, which, when embedded adequately in an organization's growth processes, can lead to material advantages for the firm and benefits for society.

The opportunity for good growth has always existed, but forming social impact markets has heightened its potential. These are markets where societal benefits rank high on the motives for advocating or purchasing products or services. These markets grow when societal issues gain prevalence among consumers, and in response, companies integrate environmental or social benefits into their offerings. For instance, the fashion industry has been increasingly impacted by a plethora of practices contributing to a massive accumulation of waste. The World Economic Forum reported that approximately 1 percent of clothes are recycled today around the world. Many end up in what are becoming vast mountains of disposed clothes. Importantly, these findings are communicated not only in scientific papers or analyst reports, but also in the form of a fashion show portraying famous models on Instagram[3]. In other words, organizations fighting for sustainability actions are becoming savvier in their methods to increase relevance, attention, and engagement by the public— all of which stimulate the formation of markets for products that respond to the societal issue like brands in the shoe industry such as Nothing New. By adequately weaving the ideal societal benefits into products or services, companies can accelerate the formation of social impact markets, make material contributions to societal needs, and gain competitive advantage.

Many recent studies have reported a growing demand by consumers across product categories for societal benefits. For instance, according to a survey by McKinsey & Company[4], 66 percent of all respondents and 75 percent of millennial respondents say they consider sustainability when purchasing. They also found that 60 percent of respondents were willing to pay more for products with sustainability claims. Similarly, a study by NielsenIQ reported that 78 percent of US consumers say a sustainable lifestyle is essential to them. The Economist Intelligence Unit[5] reports that fifty-two percent of managers believe consumers are driving the increased focus on sustainability issues in the fashion and textile industry. In another signal of the presence of social impact markets, over the past five years, there has been a 71 percent rise in online searches for sustainable goods globally. Consumers engage with sustainable businesses in new ways, and not just in more developed economies. Consumer satisfaction in developing and emerging economies is also tied to concerns around climate change, and many consumers want businesses to commit to protecting nature and natural systems.

A study[6] by Deloitte Consulting published in the *Harvard Business Review* in 2023, shared the results of surveys conducted of more than 500 brands and over 30 product categories. The article describes a crucial generational change in the role of sustainability when buying products, with significantly stronger favorable effects found among younger consumers. For instance, respondents from the Gen Z generation were 27 percent more likely than older groups to purchase products when they associated the brands with a positive social impact. They propose a mechanism for the effect of sustainability associations and purchases, namely consumer trust. There is a long history of research studying the impact of trust on purchase decisions. The researchers at Deloitte, Ashley Reichheld, John Peto, and Cory Ritthaler, propose that sustainability associations impact purchases via their effect on trust. Academic researchers have also found this connection, providing a more complete explanation for how investments in social impact can result in commercial advantage.

Despite claims of growing customer interest in societal benefits, managers would be wise to question if such reports translate to actual demand for products in their specific categories. The gap between claims and actual behavior in sustainability is a common challenge faced by government officials, non-profit organizations, and companies interested in social impact work. Consumers regularly claim interest in societal benefits, but when those products become available, they don't align with expectations, leaving managers disappointed and discouraged. Yet the root cause of this sustainability gap is not so much with the customer, but with the managers and research methods they use to study market demand. The study of social impact benefits can be at risk of what psychologists and sociologists call Social Desirability Bias—the tendency of participants to answer moral or ethical questions in ways consistent with socially acceptable responses rather than expressing their true beliefs or behaviors. This form of bias is commonly present when conducting research related to social impact and can lead to overestimation of market interest. In the chapter on research practices, we will present ways managers can mitigate this effect and establish a more accurate read into the size and potential of social impact markets in their industry.

However, market research reports are not the only indications of a growing demand for societal benefits in products and services. There are more robust signals of the presence of social impact markets, notably, the growth in revenue and market position of products and services that have taken the step to compete on social impact. On November 6, 2019 Unilever made an announcement that sent shockwaves through the sustainability profession. The CEO reported that their portfolio of brands with social impact benefits, what they called "purpose-led," was growing 69 percent faster than the rest of the business and delivering 75 percent of the company's total growth. In addition, seven of their top ten brands were all brands that embedded social impact in their value proposition. These included Dove, whose Real Beauty program celebrating women's authentic selves helped drive ten consecutive years of revenue and profit growth, and Lifebuoy soap, whose global handwashing campaign to reduce disease fueled a 17 percent annual sales growth rate over three years.

Still, Unilever is hardly a monopoly when competing on social impact. Consider the case of Allbirds, which sold one million pairs of "planet-friendly" shoes in two years and achieved a $1.9 billion valuation three years after launch. They positioned the brand on a combination of personal and societal benefits. Yes, they are comfortable, lightweight, and unique. However, they are also produced with some of the industry's lowest carbon emissions. The combination of personal and social impact makes Allbirds challenging to emulate and compete with. Another well-known case of good growth is Patagonia, which saw revenue grow more than 30 percent following a campaign promoting sustainable buying and recycling of clothing. Blueland's green cleaning products have experienced 800 percent year-on-year growth since the brand's launch in 2019, partly because of the elimination of plastic in household cleaning products. In a different type of example, MrBeast, the YouTube-based celebrity, has built one of the largest individual platforms, accumulating 240 million subscribers. His videos are a collection of creative and unexpected stunts that cost between $100,000 to $300,000 to produce and, in 2023, earned him a reported $600 million in revenue. In 2022 he applied the same model of videos to social impact stunts. In one, they re-built an orphanage in South Africa to save it from closing. They have built power stations and schools in remote villages and provided access to food to hundreds in need. Over time, his social impact work has become inextricably linked to his entertainment work, making him a new type of celebrity that fuses both efforts. These examples, which include decades-old brands as well as newer startups and industry disruptors, provide evidence that social impact markets exist in real and valuable ways. Still, individual cases are not enough to establish the general presence of a market trend. For that, we and other researchers have studied general consumer behavior across hundreds of products, multiple countries, and different categories.

A meta-analysis by Huang, Sim, and Zhao published in 2019 by the *International Review of Finance Analysis* analyzed 437 studies across different countries, all measuring the effect of corporate social responsibility investments on the financial performance of firms. In this case, they accounted for other economic fluctuations and conditions impacting financial performance, therefore gaining a more transparent view into the effect of social impact investments. They found a positive and significant effect in 86 percent of the studies, with a null effect in 12 percent and a negative impact in the remaining 2 percent.

The GlobalData service consolidates information about new products introduced across 20 leading economies. The data provides insights into the expansion of social impact offerings. For instance, the percentage of new consumer-packaged goods products with social impact claims, be it environmentally friendly, fair trade, or biodegradable ingredients, has doubled over the last decade. In addition, between 2018 and 2023, one of every three new packaging designs and formats for consumer-packaged goods products carried a sustainability claim. In European countries, that percentage climbed to 42 percent.

An industry report by NielsenIQ and McKinsey analyzed sales data across 600,000 products in 32 consumer-packaged goods categories. Using the codes generated by scanner data during supermarket purchases, Nielsen can measure the types of product claims present on labels. With this data, they established 93 different product features related to social impact including "fair trade," "organic," "eco-friendly," and "biodegradable," among others. The team created six categories of social impact based on the claims: animal welfare, environmental sustainability, organic farming methods, plant-based ingredients, social responsibility, and sustainable packaging. Using a longitudinal study with five years of data starting in 2017, they investigated the effect of social impact claims on growth by conducting a multivariate regression analysis controlling for other factors that influence the growth rate of products, such as the life cycle, price, or prior market share. In their findings, the authors state:

> Over the past five years, products making ESG-related claims accounted for 56 percent of all growth—about 18 percent more than would have been expected given their standing at the beginning of the five years: products making these claims averaged 28 percent cumulative growth over the five years, versus 20 percent for products that made no such claims. As for the CAGR, products with ESG-related claims boasted a 1.7 percentage-point advantage—a significant amount in a mature and modestly growing industry— over products without them. Products making ESG-related claims, therefore, now account for nearly half of all retail sales in the categories examined.

Despite the positive average effects of ESG claims on product growth, there was significant variation in the product growth rate with ESG claims across different categories. As illustrated in Figure 1.1 from the published report, we see some categories, such as paper and plastic products, bath and shower

Growth differential vs prevalence of ESG1-related claims by product category

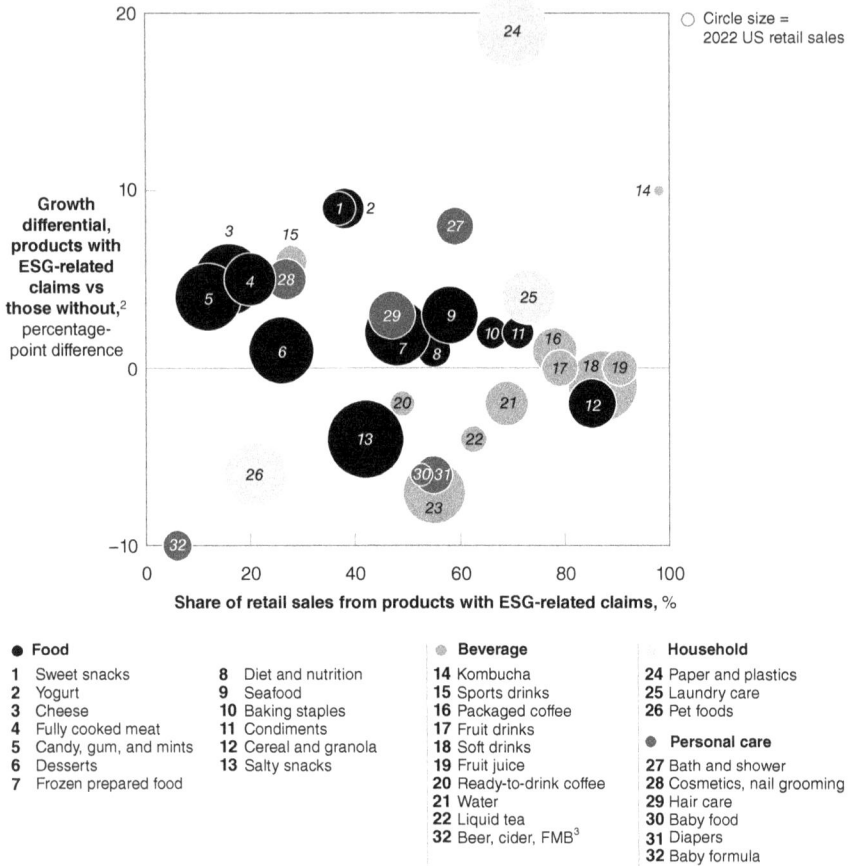

Food

1	Sweet snacks	8	Diet and nutrition
2	Yogurt	9	Seafood
3	Cheese	10	Baking staples
4	Fully cooked meat	11	Condiments
5	Candy, gum, and mints	12	Cereal and granola
6	Desserts	13	Salty snacks
7	Frozen prepared food		

Beverage

14 Kombucha
15 Sports drinks
16 Packaged coffee
17 Fruit drinks
18 Soft drinks
19 Fruit juice
20 Ready-to-drink coffee
21 Water
22 Liquid tea
32 Beer, cider, FMB[3]

Household

24 Paper and plastics
25 Laundry care
26 Pet foods

Personal care

27 Bath and shower
28 Cosmetics, nail grooming
29 Hair care
30 Baby food
31 Diapers
32 Baby formula

[1] Environmental, social, and governance.
[2] Difference between June 2018–June 2022 CAGR growth for products with ESG-related claims vs those without.
[3] Flavored malt beverages.
Source: NielsenIQ

McKinsey & Company

Figure 1.1 Prevalence and performance of environmental, social, and governance-related claims vary by product category.

products, and yogurt, where products with social impact are outgrowing products without social impact by ten percentage points or more.

Just as important, the data finds categories such as pet food or beer, where products with social impact are experiencing slower growth than those without it. These findings suggest that integrating social impact into a brand or product needs to be managed with a similar level of strategy and planning as other innovation initiatives. Claiming social impact alone is not enough to fuel good growth.

An NYU Stern Center for Sustainable Business initiative study found results consistent with the NielsenIQ/McKinsey report. Looking at sustainability-related claims on more than 70,000 consumer products, the study reported 16 percent growth in dollar sales over five years, representing $114 billion in revenue and accounting for 50 percent of CPG-industry growth at a rate three times faster than that of the total CPG market. But again, the relationship between social impact benefits and market share of products varied significantly by category.

Our research on both large and small firms shows a gain from sustainable new product introductions, with large firms gaining over $260 million and smaller firms gaining between $30 million–$200 million in market value on average. In a separate study, we partnered with the Modern Marketing Association (MMA) to survey 5,000 customers in the United States to understand the importance of social impact relative to other foundational and more modern benefits offered by different industry segments. There were 22 different benefit types organized across six categories: affordability, convenience, personalization, functionality, meaning, and social impact. We did not ask consumers to declare their preferences for different benefit types to avoid the social desirability bias. Instead, we used a discrete choice model to estimate the importance to consumers of different benefits in the specific choice of a product or service across seven types of industries: airlines, quick service restaurants, non-alcoholic beverages, hotels, general merchandise stores, department stores, and personal care products. We defined a social impact customer as one that prioritizes societal benefits among their top 5 criteria for purchase. Based on consumer-declared preferences, the average size of the social impact customer segment across the industries in our study is 33 percent, significantly below the market size estimates generated by industry reports. Still, this number suggests that about 1/3 of the market across industries prioritizes social impact in their purchase, even after considering other benefits. Figure 1.2 has a more detailed look into the data which finds that the market size of social impact customers varies significantly by industry and age.

Consistent with other industry findings, our research suggests that while there are social impact customers of every age, the most significant incidence is among the younger generations. In the case of department stores and non-alcoholic beverages, the size of the social impact market reaches over 50 percent.

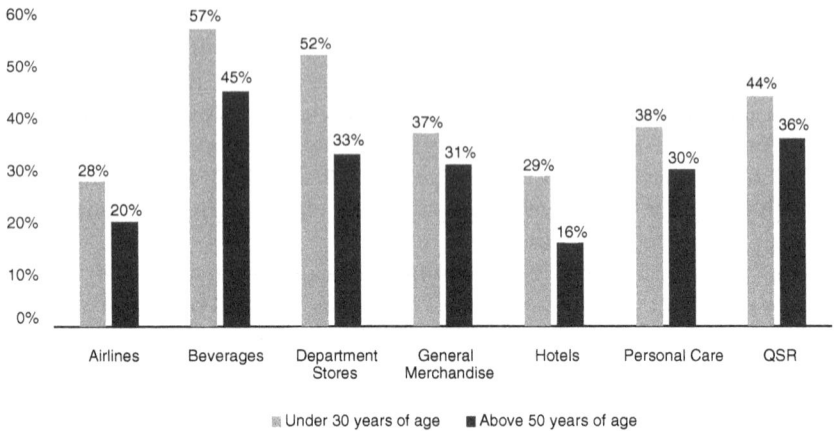

Figure 1.2 Percentage of social impact customers by industry.

Managers must prioritize among different types of benefits to offer customers. That decision is essential in their ability to establish a value proposition that fits the needs of their market. Therefore, we studied the importance of social impact relative to other benefits managers could focus on. As expected, affordability and quality still dominate across industries and age groups. However, an exciting finding emerged in the contrast between convenience and social impact. Illustrated in Figure 1.3, their relationship seems to be in opposing directions. Notice that as age increases, the value of convenience dominates the value of social impact. For customers over 50, convenience is a predominant driver of purchase.

A different picture emerges among younger customers. The gap reduces and, in some industries, inverts, with social impact becoming a more critical purchase driver than convenience.

Finally, in one of our studies[7], we examined where growth for a product with a social benefit originates, whether from the cannibalization of conventional products, from competitive social benefit products, or the expansion of the market. In our exploration of the detergent category with Nielsen data, we found that after 16 weeks, 87 percent of the sales came from expansion of the market and new customers, as opposed to cannibalization or competition.

The research findings described in this chapter lead to several important conclusions. First, that social impact markets exist. This means some customers prioritize social impact benefits in their purchase decisions, and those customers are driving growth across many industries. We call this type of growth "good growth" because it is provoked by the combination of

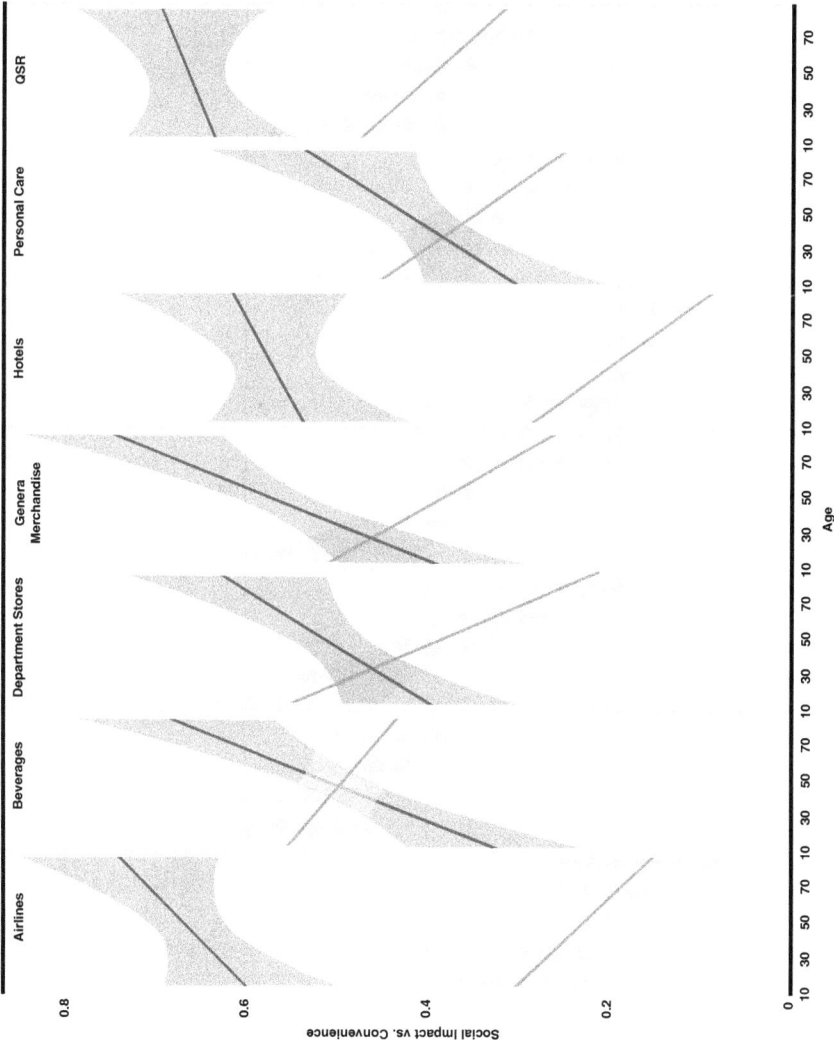

Figure 1.3 Comparison of the importance of convenience versus social impact-related benefits across age groups.

personal and societal benefits. Second, it is important to note that the effect of social impact markets is not equally distributed. Secondary research analysis and primary research studies both find that social impact benefits do not motivate all customers in the same way. Additionally, the studies show a more significant influence on the growth of some product categories than others. Therefore, like many other benefits that managers can choose from, social impact has the potential of being either a driver of choice or an irrelevant factor. As a result, managers should apply the same rigor, strategic thinking, and careful planning to integrate social impact into their products and services that they apply to other opportunities in managing their growth. That is precisely our aim with this book, to equip managers with the tools to conduct the correct type of analysis, research, and discussions that can lead to more effective integration of social impact into their market offerings.

Notes

1 University of Montreal (2009, March 13). Fridges And Washing Machines Liberated Women, Study Suggests. *ScienceDaily*.
2 Murphy, H. (2020, March 13). Why Soap Works. *The New York Times*.
3 Instagram (n.d.). [Instagram Reel]. Retrieved from www.instagram.com/reel/C8C11a1BBes/?igsh=MWYzdGJhYXhyaGhxOA.
4 McKinsey & Company (2020). Consumers care about sustainability—and back it up with their wallets.
5 Economist Intelligence Unit (2022). Is sustainability in fashion?. Economist Intelligence Unit.
6 HBR Editors (2023, September). Research: Consumers' sustainability demands are rising. *Harvard Business Review*.
7 Youngtak Kim and Sundar Bharadwaj (2023). "Environmental and Social Claims in New Products and Financial Performance." Working Paper, University of Tennessee.

Chapter 2

Understanding Social Impact

When you think about Social Impact, what comes to mind? The Center for Social Impact defines it as *the net effect of an activity on a community and the well-being of individuals and families.* The Michigan Ross Center for Social Impact defines it as *"a significant, positive change that addresses a pressing social challenge."* A prompt on ChatGPT says that *"social impact refers to the effect or influence that an individual, organization, project, or initiative has on the well-being and development of society."* It is essential to notice a few aspects of these definitions. First, it's not specific to a particular area of impact. Social impact could relate to environmental issues such as climate change or plastic pollution, or social problems such as racial justice, education, or health and wellness. Second, it refers to actions the organization is trying to address. This is an essential point because managers often think about actions relating to the financial goals they are trying to achieve when working in a company. Did the brand grow? Did it sell more than the prior period? Did it have the right level of profitability? Did the team operate at the right speed or quality? Yet, these definitions invite us to think about consequences beyond financial performance. They introduce implications for society at large and in specific communities. The definitions invite us to think about the consequences of a business beyond its direct responsibility for driving shareholder value and growth. For instance, do our actions, our products, or our services have a negative or positive impact on society? And if they do, how does that influence our ability to grow?

Seeking to compete on social impact starts with clarifying what managers are trying to do. Many terms used in the area of sustainability can generate confusion. You have social entrepreneurship, social business, impact investment, ESG, purpose, corporate social responsibility, cause marketing, social enterprise, and social innovation. At times, these terms are used interchangeably, but they define different aspects of the broader sustainability field. Some are more non-profit in nature; some are more for-profit in nature. Some are more geared towards driving business outcomes. Some are more geared towards reducing risks. Some are more geared towards managing the corporate reputation. In this book, we define the efforts of

DOI: 10.4324/9781003383246-3

competing on social impact *as the capability to drive customer demand by creating tangible and meaningful societal benefits.* The ideal way to generate customer demand is by creating benefits that customers value and competitors lack, while also contributing to a pricing advantage. With these three elements, you are likely to grow at a profit that allows you to expand the benefits offered as well as your social impact.

In essence, we're examining how to compete with benefits that help a brand win with a positive social impact. However, when thinking about product benefits, managers tend to focus on cost, quality, or convenience. Brands compete by being either the affordable option, the best quality option, or the most convenient option. When competing on social impact, you add a fourth layer of benefits—consequence—which are the implications to the customer or society at large of purchasing your option vs. the alternative. Managing consequences is a new form of generating customer utility and stimulating purchases.

The traditional training on growth management focuses on designing products around customer needs and optimizing the utility that those products can create at the moment of purchase or usage. When managing products or services, managers rarely consider the societal consequences of their choices because they are not trained to do so. However, in some cases, not always, not in every industry, not every situation, but increasingly, there are more and more instances where the societal consequences of your product benefits can become a source of customer utility.

Translating your social impact into a part of your offering can generate a new advantage. That is at the core of what we mean by finding good growth. How do we generate customer demand by offering benefits responsive to societal needs and not just individual needs?

Consider examples of companies trying to embed social impact benefits into their offerings. Part of the reason for reviewing many examples is to make the point that social impact efforts are everywhere, like new technologies such as GenAI. Sometimes, we don't notice them, but they are prevalent across many product categories and industries. As you review them, think about what could explain some of the differences in approach. First, consider the investment by Budweiser in 2019 to announce their shift to renewable energy during their manufacturing process. They created an advertising message and aired it during the Super Bowl to announce the use of wind-generated energy. Another brand of beer, Stella Artois, created a program in partnership with the non-profit organization water.org to support access to clean water by donating proceeds from selling Stella branded chalices. Domino's Pizza called for donations for children's cancer research while paying for an order. L'Oréal launched a digital advertising campaign to announce its efforts to reduce the environmental impact of its business operations, which includes protecting water, nourishing biodiversity, and reducing plastics. As you explore the examples in the table in Figure 2.1, I hope you can see more clearly the breadth of social impact activity that regularly takes place in the marketplace. Yet, are all these the same, or do they differ in meaningful ways?

While all these examples carry a social impact element, they are distinct in two important ways. The first is the level of the action. Is the social impact activity occurring at the company or the product level? Investments like those promoted in the Citibank or L'Oréal campaigns are companywide efforts unrelated to specific brands or products in their portfolio. That means they are two steps removed from the customer experience and more likely directed to other stakeholders such as investors or employees. In

Brand	Demand Side Action	Type of Benefit
Budweiser	Superbowl ad announcing the adoption of renewable energy in production.	Environmental – Expanding Clean Energy Use
H&M	Program to reuse or recycle used clothes.	Environmental – Waste Management
Coca-Cola	Outdoor advertising serves as an air filter, absorbing pollutants.	Environmental – Clean Air
Citi	Display an advertising campaign to promote the donation of funds to the "No Kid Hungry" organization when using Citi-branded credit cards at restaurants.	Social – Reducing Child Hunger
KLM Airlines	Fly Responsibly campaign to promote transportation or communication that does not involve air travel to reduce carbon emissions.	Environmental – Expanding Clean Energy Use
L'Oreal	Display ad campaign promoting the company's action to reduce its environmental footprint and protect biodiversity.	Environment – Reduce pollution
Stella Artois	Promotion to donate proceeds from the sale of a Stella Artois branded chalice to support the work of water.org in expanding access to clean water.	Environmental – Expanding Water Access
Newman's Own	Common Good wine is donating 100% of after-tax profits to charity through Newman's Own Foundation, a private nonprofit that supports child-focused programs.	Social – Children Nutrition
Domino's Pizza	This allows customers to donate to St. Jude Hospital, which supports cancer research when paying for an online order.	Social – Cancer Research
Autodesk	Development of an "Insight" tool enabling architects and engineers to increase energy efficiency in their buildings with real-time environmental performance analysis.	Environment – Increasing Energy Efficiency
Rubicon	Waste management company enabling mid-size businesses to reduce the use of landfills and increase the amount of recycled waste.	Environmental – Waste Management
Allbirds	Sustainable footwear with production processes and material usage that lowers carbon footprint and waste.	Environmental – Reduced Emission and Waste

Figure 2.1 Social impact examples across brands and industries.

contrast, Allbirds or Domino's work is happening at the product level, and therefore, they are a more direct component of the experience that customers have with the brand. The second dimension is the centrality of the social impact work to the product offering. In the case of Budweiser and renewable energy, that action is not central to the product or its historical positioning. To the best of our knowledge, that action marked the first time that Budweiser communicated in a mainstream and large-scale way about renewable energy in their manufacturing. The brand had issued sporadic posts related to recycling cans, but the presence of an environmental message was not central to the way they compete. Therefore, consumers are unlikely to associate Budweiser with a brand actively involved in environmental causes. However, in the case of Atlanta-based waste management technology company Rubicon, reducing landfill waste is core to their value proposition to customers and their mission as a company. That societal benefit is almost inseparable from other cost or logistical benefits they offer. As illustrated by Figure 2.2, combining level and centrality provides a way of understanding essential differences in the management of social impact investments.

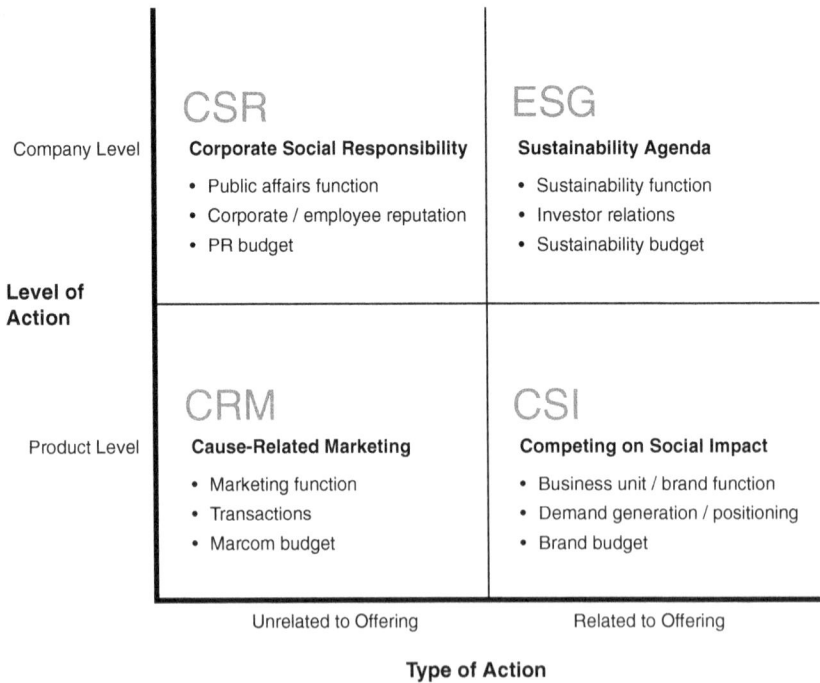

Company Level	**CSR** **Corporate Social Responsibility** • Public affairs function • Corporate / employee reputation • PR budget	**ESG** **Sustainability Agenda** • Sustainability function • Investor relations • Sustainability budget
Level of Action		
Product Level	**CRM** **Cause-Related Marketing** • Marketing function • Transactions • Marcom budget	**CSI** **Competing on Social Impact** • Business unit / brand function • Demand generation / positioning • Brand budget
	Unrelated to Offering	Related to Offering

Type of Action

Figure 2.2 Map of social impact initiatives based on their level of action (company vs. product) and centrality to brand value.

The upper left quadrant is composed of more traditional corporate social responsibility activities. Those tend to be at the company level and are frequently in areas that matter to the employees or communities but are not necessarily directly related to the product offerings. Examples of these activities include The Coca-Cola Company air filtering billboard or their vast reforestation efforts in Mexico. They are company-level initiatives not central to their value proposition to consumers. Such actions are essential for stakeholder management, employee relations and corporate reputation. Therefore they tend to be managed by the public affairs or public relations function and should have little to no presence in their market activities with customers. In the upper right quadrant are company-level efforts central to the product or business. These will likely be managed as part of the firm's sustainability or ESG agenda. Their goal often combines risk management, cost management, and investor relations. They represent activities that tend to focus on the supply side of the business and can cover both environmental and social initiatives. However, these actions rarely elicit the interest of the customer or directly translate into marketplace benefits. They may generate goodwill but not buy will. Hence, they should not actively participate in demand-creation efforts and investments. In the lower left quadrant are cause-related marketing efforts. These are actions at the product level, often tied to a transaction but not intended to be part of the brand positioning or value proposition. They amount to acts of generosity or philanthropy by a brand, frequently via messages at the moment of purchase. These activities include the chalice promotion by Stella Artois, the donation of proceeds to water.org, or the promotion by Publix supermarkets to ask for small donations to support their food drive in local communities. They are customer-facing but tactical and short-lived. As a result, they are easy to emulate, offer limited differentiation, and tend not to last multiple budgeting cycles.

There is a long history of cause-related marketing efforts, starting with the promotion by American Express back in the 1980s to donate a penny toward the restoration of the Statue of Liberty every time a customer used one of its credit cards. The project generated $1.7 million for the Statue project and a substantial increase in usage of the American Express card, according to a report by *The New York Times*. Importantly, these programs did not alter the brand's position in the market, nor did they have long-lasting impacts on its competitiveness.

The lower right quadrant is different. These investments and actions occur at a product level and are closely tied to the product offering, which represent new benefits intended to differentiate brands and build demand for products. These actions are examples of the pursuit for Good Growth— companies using social impact to compete in the marketplace in different and better ways. Their presence in the market is not new; their origins can be traced back to the work of entrepreneurs like Anita Roddick, Yvon Chouinard, and Ray C. Anderson. Anita started the Body Shop with a mission to create personal care products in ways that protected animals and the environment. Yvon founded Patagonia in the early 1970s and built the business with environmental protection as a central aspect of its value proposition. Finally, Ray founded Interface and grew it to become the world's largest carpet tile manufacturer. In the early 1990s he began a total transformation of the business to significantly reduce its carbon emissions and make waste reduction and recycling a core benefit of their offerings. For brands like Body Shop, Patagonia, or Interface, social impact was a core motivator for their business and a defining characteristic of their market position. It gave them a reason to be different, and, in many cases, it was a driver of choice for their product. Finding Good Growth required their companies to operate in ways that resembled a hybrid organization—partly for profit because they continued their aim of maximizing shareholder value, and partly for non-profit because they were just as motivated by a societal mission as a financial one. This made it credible to outside stakeholders and difficult for other firms to emulate, resulting in a competitive advantage.

The role of this framework is to help managers think with greater clarity about the nature of the social impact work their brand or firm is doing and the role it can play in its demand chain. When these distinctions are not established, it is possible to confuse an excellent firm-facing action with an ill-advised customer-facing action. Consider the earlier example of Budweiser and its 2019 Superbowl ad announcing its use of renewable energy in production. At that time, a 30-second advertisement during the game cost approximately $5 million, given the large and widespread audience it reaches. Therefore, this is not a trivial decision. It is a very visible and important one for their marketing team, which then begs the question of why a firm would invest so much in generating awareness about an action that arguably has little to do with their brand and the reasons most people buy their product. There are other reasons to communicate sustainability-related changes in your supply chain, such as influencing stakeholder perceptions and investors or even motivating employees. But it is hard to justify the investment behind a Super Bowl ad to achieve goals that are not related to driving demand for a product – the opportunity cost is too high. Still, it is common for firms to want to communicate their social impact deeds broadly in the name of corporate reputation or in response to external calls for action. In fact, research has found that one of the antecedents of corporate social responsibility investments is stakeholder pressure[1]. Leaders facing calls for change in one area of their operations might look to communicate good deeds in other areas to defend or protect their company's reputation. At times, they might also wonder if making customers aware of the social responsibility actions would lead to greater engagement or willingness to buy their products. One of us was a part of the first sustainability strategy taskforce at The Coca-Cola Company. As part of that project, the team aimed to create a communication campaign to increase awareness among consumers about the different ways in which the company contributed to society. Called "Live Positively," it included a visual identity system and a series of advertisements for the brand. The messages were emotional and optimistic in tone and highlighted the company's work protecting the environment, helping communities, and contributing to education and other areas. They were uplifting for employees to see. However, their impact on consumers and their choices for company products was negligent. Eventually, the social impact efforts continued, but investments in communicating them to consumers were redirected to other activities. Research has found that the relationship between CSR and consumer purchases is complex and highly dependent on the firm type and the nature of the CSR activity (Nickerson et al., 2021)[2]. Otherwise, communicating CSR actions to customers can amount to wasted demand-side resources because they rarely help the firm enhance its competitive position in the market. Going back to our example of Budweiser, their message about the use of renewable energy has little to do with the taste of their beer, their brand heritage, or the negative externalities that beer companies might be known for. The fact that they are transforming their supply chain to reduce carbon emissions should be celebrated. However, the fact that they are bringing that message to their consumers should be questioned. Resources that touch the customer should prioritize areas of demand and value creation, and it is not clear that renewable energy will be one for a brand like Budweiser.

Alternatively, firms operating in the CSI quadrant can merge customer needs with social impact benefits in ways that generate competitive advantage. A case in point is Autodesk, a leading design, engineering, and construction software provider. Their building performance analysis software, which includes Building Information Modeling, enables architects and designers to simulate energy use and material requirements, which are core to green building design. These features create a direct social impact via the management of environmental footprints while at the same time generating economic benefits for the user and a competitive advantage for Autodesk. Is this action an example of corporate social responsibility? Or is this an example of business as usual? It is both. The company's product innovation enabling green construction and design is part of its sustainability report. Still, it is also a critical product feature that helps it compete in the market. That duality of purpose is a defining characteristic of brands that are competing on social impact and achieving good growth.

While we have used several examples related to environmental causes, social impact is not limited to environmental programs. Actions that serve to advance any of the 17 United Nations Sustainable Development Goals[3] can be considered a social impact investment. For instance, the retailer Target has taken bold steps to compete on social impact in the area of inclusion.

Imagine that you are buying toys for your kids or a friend, and you go to the Target website. You will notice something different about the way they present the toy options on the site. The organizational structure of toy products in most retailers used to be by gender—toys for boys and toys for girls. In 2015 Target announced a decision to stop organizing their toys by gender to create a more inclusive environment for all children, including those that do not conform to traditional binary gender identities. At the time of their decision, they faced criticism on social media based on the signs in their store—including the example in Figure 2.3, where they separated placement of toys by gender categories without a particular reason.

Today, the gender-neutral organizing structure allows shoppers the freedom to find themselves in the product, creating a more inclusive environment for all and sending a message of support to the LGBTQ+ community. Target's commitment to inclusive customer experience goes beyond gender identity. It is present in many other details and decisions that shape their in-store and website experience. For instance, when you go to a store, who are the people often selected to serve as models for the clothes or products the company is selling? Next time you visit a Target store, notice the intentional inclusion and representation in their portrayal of people in their store displays across gender, race, and physical abilities. How often have you seen people with disabilities highlighted as the people

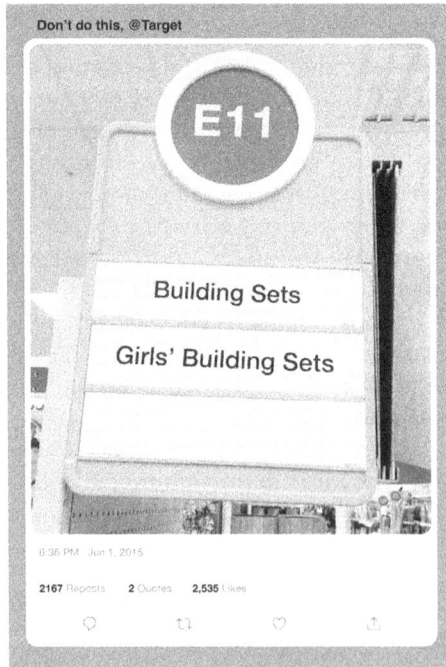

Figure 2.3 Example of social media post criticizing Target's product organization in stores.

showcasing a product in a store? The visibility of people with disabilities in our overall cultural experience is very low. Target is changing that in their in-store environment, contributing to the promotion of greater inclusion, which is an aspect of the UN Sustainable Development Goals. At the same time, it is done in a way that integrates seamlessly into the shopper experience and, therefore, is a part of how they compete in the market.

Another brand competing on social impact is Allbirds. If you don't know about Allbirds, please stop reading, go online, and check them out. Launched in 2016 by Tim Brown and Joey Zwillinger, a biotech engineer with expertise in renewable materials, the company introduced a shoe that was distinct not only because of its looks and comfort but also because of its materials and reduced carbon footprint. Their product became a staple of the startup business environment and achieved dramatic growth driven in part by an environmental benefit that was largely absent in their industry. The entry of Allbirds amounted to a type of market disruption in the footwear industry because they captured significant yet mainly uncontested growth for a period of time due to their unique value proposition was

Figure 2.4 Examples of guest inclusion efforts by Target.

appealing to a segment of the market but difficult for competitors to emulate. The value proposition started with comfort and design, but also included the element of sustainability, specifically around the materials used in the manufacturing process. If you go to the website, you will see how they merge functional benefits, such as close fit and comfort, with environmental benefits in terms of their reduced carbon footprint and materials. It is not a message of corporate social responsibility. It is a message of performance through the lens of social impact.

In a final example, imagine you go into Starbucks looking for a sweet snack around three in the afternoon. Some of your options are captured in the picture below. You can get chocolate with hazelnut butter, dark chocolate expresso beans, or a life-saving snack bar. What would you choose? This is one of the most direct positionings on social impact we have found in the market. Designed with a mission to combat hunger across the globe, the brand was introduced in 2013 by actors Kristen Bell, Ryan Devlin, Todd Grinnell, and Ravi Patel. Since its launch, the company has donated more than 30 million packets of nutrient-dense Plumpy'Nut to children in need. It has also expanded beyond snack bars with product lines, including kids' snacks, granola, and oatmeal, which are available at major retailers, including Whole Foods, Kroger, Nordstrom, and Caribou Coffee.

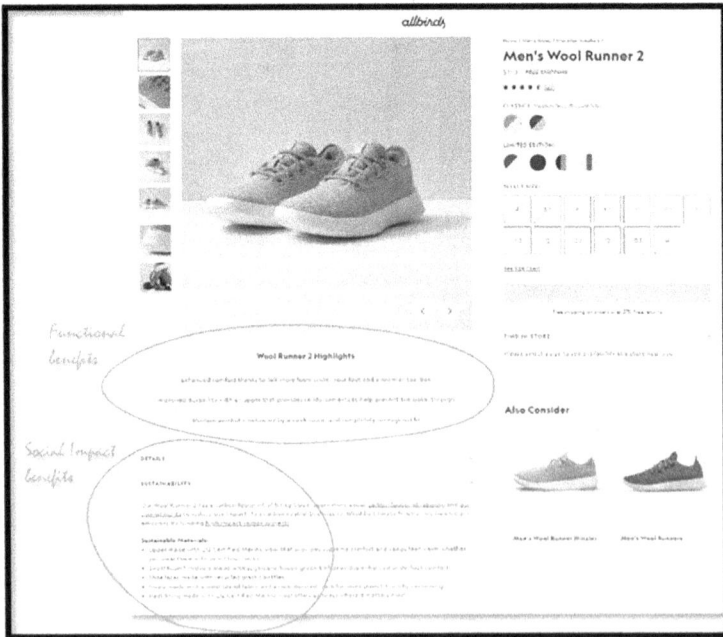

Figure 2.5 Allbirds' product description on the brand website.

Figure 2.6 Example of the snack brand "This Bar Saves Lives".
Notice that product features, such as taste, ingredients, or nutritional benefits, play a secondary role in the social benefit of their presentation. As in the case of Target, AutoCad, or Allbirds, This Bar Saves Lives is competing on social impact, making a societal benefit core to the reason consumers should purchase.

As you reflect on the examples discussed earlier, there are important distinctions that separate efforts to compete on social impact from other ways in which a firm may act to advance a sustainability agenda. First, the integration of the social impact benefit happens at the product or service level, not at the company level. The audience is focused on customers, users, or consumers of the product and less so on other non-commercial stakeholders like employees or regulators. The social impact benefits are designed to be central to the value proposition and a point of difference for the brand. They intend to create a material and meaningful societal benefit while at the same time enhancing the competitive position and creating demand among specific market segments. The resources to manage the social impact benefit come from the brand or product teams and budgets, and their actions tend to be ongoing, not tactical or sporadic. Finally, the measurement of success is not only goodwill or reputational gains, but also the influence on customer decisions to buy and the contribution to societal needs. As a result, when competing on social impact, managers integrate societal benefits into the customer experience as if they were another feature or attribute of their product.

We combine the different criteria discussed above to form an assessment that can help categorize a firm's social impact activity and determine the more appropriate course of action and management approach. Scores below 20 would indicate that the actions are closer to traditional corporate social responsibility. Scores above 40 suggest the brand is, in fact, competing on social impact. The rest of the book can help guide the strategies and implementation of social impact efforts to achieve good growth.

Area of Action	Corporate Social Responsibility	Scale	Competing on Social Impact
Level	Company or Business Unit	1 2 3 4 5 6 7	Product or Service
Audience	Stakeholders (e.g., employees, investors, regulators, NGOs)	1 2 3 4 5 6 7	Customers (e.g., users, buyers, sellers)
Role	Social benefit unrelated to the core business	1 2 3 4 5 6 7	Social benefit central to the core business
Intent	Risk management, Reputation management, or Cost management	1 2 3 4 5 6 7	Differentiation, Positioning, and Demand Creation
Resources	Budget from the sustainability, investor relations, or public relations teams	1 2 3 4 5 6 7	Budget from the brand or product teams
Duration	Tactical and short-term	1 2 3 4 5 6 7	On-going
KPIs	Goodwill – reputation, risk reduction.	1 2 3 4 5 6 7	Buywill – brand preference, purchase.
Action	Focus on targeted communications to stakeholder audiences (not customers).	1 2 3 4 5 6 7	Integrate into customer experience and communication efforts.

Figure 2.7 Social impact assessment.

Notes

1 Santini, Fernando de Oliveira et al. (2021). Antecedents and consequences of corporate social responsibility: a meta-analysis. *Journal of Social Marketing, 11*(3): 278–305.
2 Nickerson, Dionne, Lowe, Michael, Pattabhiramaiah, Adithya, & Sorescu, Alina (2022). The Impact of Corporate Social Responsibility on Brand Sales: An Accountability Perspective. *Journal of Marketing, 86*(2), 5–28.
3 United Nations (n.d.). *Sustainable Development Goals.* United Nations Department of Economic and Social Affairs.

Chapter 3

Necessity or Distraction?

Imagine for a moment that your company decides to support reforestation efforts in one of the communities in which it operates, and you are asked to lead the initiative. The first step you take is to reach out to a local non-profit that serves your community's needs in that area to plan the requirements for collaboration and determine the necessary funds. Given that your business is not directly related to planting trees, the non-profit team will serve as the logistical arm, working with government officials to determine the best tree species and recruiting volunteers for multiple tree-planting events. Your brand will sponsor the effort, providing part of the financial resources required for the project. You then create special messages to promote the program and associate your company with the reforestation initiative, launching a campaign on social media where you post images of the volunteers wearing shirts with your brand's logo while planting the trees. At the end of the event, a total of 5,000 trees are planted, and you promote that accomplishment further on your social media channels. You feel great about what you and your company did and talk to your family and friends about it with a sense of pride.

Then, you get an email from the non-profit organization that partnered with you. They are thankful for the support and excited for the work you did together. But they are writing to ask you about the following year's plan. You realize then that it is not clear how this effort will continue. Was this a one-time shot at social impact? Should you renew the support? And if so, for how long? Are you now expected to continue supporting this effort in perpetuity? Also, should you try to plant 5,000 more trees next year? Are 5,000 trees even enough? Do you need 10,000, or would only 100,000 do? How would you even determine how many trees would be enough? And importantly, were the time and resources spent on this program helping you advance your market position? How would you even know?

This is a realistic scenario many managers face at the start of their social impact efforts. It was very close to the case of a marketing manager at a Fortune 500 company we met a few years ago. Struggling to define the boundaries of a social impact benefit, he met with us to explore the potential

DOI: 10.4324/9781003383246-4

for social impact in one of his company's brands. Halfway through the discussion, he started asking very reasonable questions about the boundary conditions of social impact. "Isn't it the case that more would always be better? And if so, how much good do we need to do?" "How many trees do I need to plant? Or how many rivers do I need to help clean? Is three enough? Do I need to clean ten? All of them?". His questions were getting to a core challenge of social impact, the risk that in the pursuit of doing good, a team might get distracted from their responsibility towards growth.

Is creating a positive social impact benefit a requirement to compete? Or are the efforts to create societal benefits a form of distraction that can lead managers to focus on activities that are not core to their responsibility to shareholders? We are in no way arguing against the need for companies to operate in responsible ways, reduce their carbon footprint, or contribute to societal needs with some of their activities or resources. But is bringing those actions into the demand side and the customer experience truly necessary? Not everyone seems to believe so, and in fact, the greater the responsibility a manager has over the profitability and top-line growth of a business, the more likely they are to think of social impact as important but not an essential part of their job.

Advocates for social impact in business tend to rely on arguments about the desires and expectations of consumers, particularly younger ones. Many reports by consulting and research firms include statements such as "*Consumer sentiment towards, and expectations of, brands have shifted. People are increasingly wanting to know more about where their products come from and how they're made and are choosing brands that can provide this level of transparency.*"[1] However, as discussed in Chapter 1, these results are impacted by social desirability bias and can therefore, yield inaccurate estimates of market interest and demand.

In our study of thousands of consumers across 11 countries, we did not find evidence for such general claims about a mainstream demand for social impact in products. We do see an impact of societal benefits on consumer purchase decisions among some groups and in some product categories, but it is not enough to qualify as a general market description. We have also conducted dozens of interviews with chief marketing officers, marketing managers, and product managers, and we see resistance to the adoption of social impact, and for good reason. The best expression of the challenge that managers face came in the answer by the Chief Sustainability Officer of a multinational company to our question about the role of sustainability in her company. We conducted interviews with chief marketing officers and chief sustainability officers as part of our research, which later informed our Harvard Business Review article. Our goal was twofold. First it was to understand the role of sustainability efforts on large companies and then to identify specific activities and organizational factors that enable sustainability considerations to become embedded as a practice. We began the interview with a simple question, "how would you describe the role of sustainability in your business?"

She paused and then said, "*You know, sustainability for us is like our fifth wheel.*" We were fascinated and intrigued by the answer, so we quickly asked, "What do you mean by that?" to which she responded, "*Well, why do we have a fifth wheel in our cars? We have it in case of an emergency, right? An unexpected event that holds us back. And then, we have to be able to solve the problem in the short run and then keep moving. In the case of a Jeep, you have it so that others can see it because it is part of the image you might want to communicate with that car. It's visible to others.*"

In addition to risk and reputation management, she made a third and critical point out of her analogy. Managers see sustainability and social impact as the fifth wheel. After all, it's not one of the four core wheels they consider using to move the business forward. It is not in the conversation about growth. Instead, it's in conversations about risk, it's in conversations about corporate social responsibility, it's in conversations about talent recruitment. But when they had meetings about growth objectives and growth strategies, social impact was not in the room. The question is…is that the right place for it, or is that a missed opportunity? Is sustainability a distraction or a necessity for growing a modern brand and business?

In Chapter 2, we discussed a general overview of how some companies are leveraging positive social impact to accelerate their growth and gain a marketplace edge. Why, then, do so many managers still find it difficult to embrace social impact as a competitive tool? In this section, we discussed the main challenges that prevent managers from unlocking the potential of social impact.

The Structure Challenge

By associating sustainability and social impact with the fifth wheel of a car, the CSO we interviewed also made a statement about the first challenge managers faced—the challenge of structure. In many corporations, social impact work is the responsibility of a separate function outside the core business activities. At times reporting to the corporate affairs or community relations office and at other times part of sustainability or research and development teams. However, social impact is rarely embedded into business units. With structure also comes accountability and incentives. Therefore, it is easy for managers responsible for the growth of the business to perceive it as important but separate from their jobs. That is because, often, it is neither a part of their responsibilities nor integrated into the performance evaluation criteria of managers responsible for achieving sales goals. As a result, there is no clear incentive to explore social impact as a source of growth. In contrast, other potential drivers of growth, such as the adoption of new technologies, the digitalization of the business, or the pursuit of innovation, take precedence.

The Perception Challenge

In many of our conversations with growth leaders, we heard a common reaction to the notion of social impact investments; they felt like a "tax"—an imposition that cost them time and money but provided no clear benefit. They often regard these investments as corporate social responsibility efforts, a managerial distraction that may be needed for reputation management but that was unrelated to the firm's economic performance. These skewed perceptions make social-impact efforts easy for growth leaders to mentally cordon off and consider someone else's responsibility.

There is also a tendency to think of the firm's social-impact work as primarily a matter of storytelling—how to frame its sustainability narrative for consumers or other stakeholders. This mindset can lead to programs that quickly wither. It is common for managers to look at the firm's sustainability efforts, be it innovations to reduce their carbon footprint or activities to enhance their communities and wonder about the impact that such good deeds may have on the customers' inclination to do business with them. That logic has led many brands to invest resources in creating stories about their sustainability efforts. They hire specialized advertising agencies to craft emotional campaigns about their socially responsible actions. However, many of those efforts rarely incorporate insights into their customers' needs. They become company-centric instead of customer-centric investments, diverting resources into messages that might create goodwill but do not translate into buy will.

Finally, many managers often believe that consumers' claims about their interest in a brand's societal benefits don't translate into actual purchase behavior. They worry that consumers may claim to prefer products with sustainability attributes like fair-trade or recycled packages, but at the moment of purchase, they will be influenced more by factors such as price, quality, or ease of access. There is a general sense among many managers that you can't trust customers' claims about their willingness to buy on the basis of social impact. However, as we discussed earlier and will show in our research practice chapter, the claim vs. behavior gap is not necessarily a reflection of poor consumer judgment but rather of poor research methods.

Unfortunately, these skewed perceptions blind managers to the opportunities social-impact initiatives offer to disrupt existing markets or discover new ones, derailing many programs before they gain traction.

The Risk Challenge

When Gillette took a stance against "toxic masculinity" in its infamous 2019 ad, the backlash was swift. Critics attacked the company for co-opting the #MeToo movement, and droves of customers threatened to boycott the brand for bashing men. Public reactions like this reinforce many leaders' concern that social-impact efforts are high-risk and low-reward investments. They also fuel a fear of being held personally responsible for a public brand humiliation.

This chilling effect can also extend to how companies decide to share existing social-impact programs. While managers may be doing good community or environmental work, some choose to keep it quiet, fearing that promoting these efforts might invite criticism about their intentions with claims that the company is only in it for the PR or is trying to divert attention from its poor performance in other areas.

Finally, there is also a personal risk associated with performance incentives. Because social impact initiatives can have long incubation periods, and managers are measured, promoted, and incentivized primarily on short-term outcomes, they may reflexively avoid social-impact investments in favor of proven programs that deliver results more quickly.

The Knowledge Challenge

Achieving growth objectives is hard work, even if your focus is 100 percent on the customer, competition, and the marketplace. Social impact can be perceived as an additional variable to optimize and one that is different from the traditional levers. It is not just about promoting new features, gaining greater market visibility, or finding the right pricing strategy. In fact, it can introduce new complexities by being concerned about environmental or social issues, as well as their different stakeholders. Creating societal benefits introduces new questions about how to find the right area of focus, how to measure return on social impact investments, or how to engage the market in ways that are authentic and meaningful. These are all concerns that can impede action. Most business leaders in established firms have had little to no experience or formal training in social benefits strategy and program implementation. But this is complex work, and the learning curve can be steep—obstacles can sabotage well-intentioned managers early in their efforts. The knowledge gap needed to manage societal benefits creates a strong disincentive for managers to compete on social impact.

When asked, few managers would deny the importance of ESG or sustainability. In fact, they frequently acknowledge that social issues are important. Climate change is important. Racial justice is important. They feel it is important for the corporation to manage, and that's why they have a diversity, equity, and inclusion (DEI) team. That's why they have a sustainability team that accounts for carbon emissions and expands supplier diversity. These are all important actions, but not a part of their job. They see their job, as Sergio Zyman, former CMO at Coca-Cola, used to say…, is to sell more things to more customers, more often, for more money. In essence, responsible for growth. What's often underneath that general sense is a lack of understanding about how to connect social impact to the growth agenda.

Competing on social impact can seem like a lot of effort in an investment that is difficult to understand and measure, with unclear returns and a high risk of perceived backlash. The combination of these challenges leads to a reasonable barrier to adoption or the pursuit of activities that are more tactical and transactional rather than transformative. As a result, many managers responsible for growth see the pursuit of societal benefits as more of a distraction than an advantage. To settle this question, it is useful to review the empirical evidence accumulated to date. What does the research on social impact find about its link to firm or product performance? In 2015 a meta-analysis by Friede, Busch, and Bassen looked at the history of the academic literature on the relationship between ESG and financial performance by consolidating results from over 2,000 studies published between 1971 and 2015. They found a positive correlation between ESG investments and firm performance in 57 percent of the studies and a negative effect in 6 percent, with the remaining results either neutral or mixed. In essence, early evidence pointed to a strong case for the role of ESG in the financial outcomes of firms. A more recent meta-analysis by Juang, Sim, and Zhao published in 2020 found a significant and positive effect of social responsibility actions on financial performance in 86 percent of the studies. Work by Atz, Liu, Bruno, and Van Holt in 2022 surveyed 1,141 peer-reviewed papers published predominantly between 2015 and 2020. They also analyzed 27 meta-analyses that reviewed research findings on the relationship between ESG investments and firm outcomes. The results section states that *"there exists a robust and positive association between sustainability and financial performance on the firm level."* Approximately 60 percent of the studies that focused on company outcomes found a positive correlation between investments in sustainability and financial performance, with 25 percent being mixed, 9 percent neutral, and roughly 6 percent negative. Given these findings, we can think of social impact investments as similar to innovation investments. Investing in innovation is not always going to generate growth. However, it's a necessary condition because if you don't innovate, you will very likely be left behind. Most managers and companies have resources dedicated to innovation, but they know not every innovation investment will yield the expected results. Still, firms view innovation as an option that, in the net, will pay off. We can think of social impact investments in the same way. Maybe not every social impact investment is going to be effective, but if managed properly, there is increasing evidence that it can play that role in helping your brand grow.

For a different type of signal about the importance of social impact in business, in 2022 we conducted a study among marketing managers surveying marketing directors and chief growth officers in 625 companies about the factors enabling growth in their organization. As shown in the table in Figure 3.1, number one in the list was data and analytics, selected by 83 percent of respondents. This is not surprising given the critical role of new

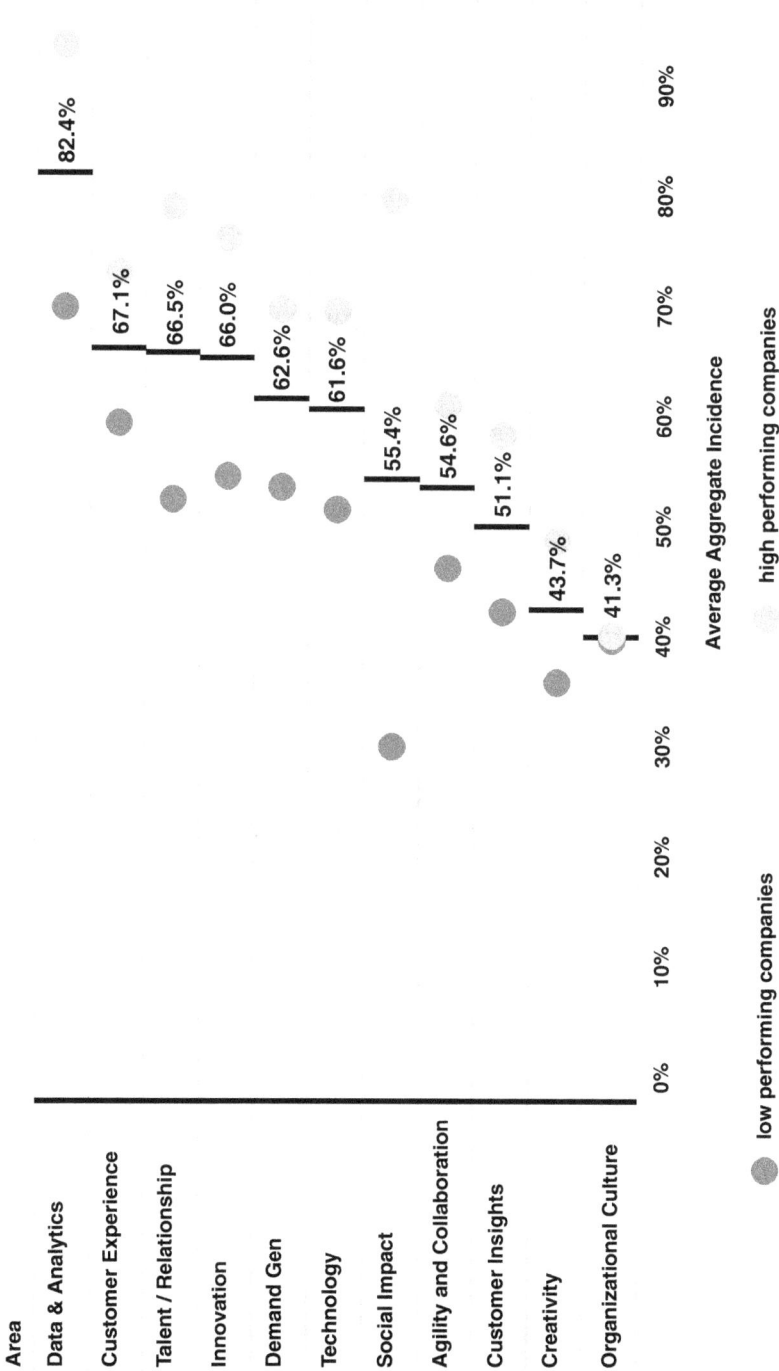

Area	
Data & Analytics	82.4%
Customer Experience	67.1%
Talent / Relationship	66.5%
Innovation	66.0%
Demand Gen	62.6%
Technology	61.6%
Social Impact	55.4%
Agility and Collaboration	54.6%
Customer Insights	51.1%
Creativity	43.7%
Organizational Culture	41.3%

0% 10% 20% 30% 40% 50% 60% 70% 80% 90%

Average Aggregate Incidence

low performing companies   high performing companies

Figure 3.1 Importance of social impact among marketing managers.

analytical tools and methods as well as the expansion of data sources available to optimize resources and investments. It was followed by managing the customer experience. Then it's talent and relationships, then innovation. Social impact was not ranked among the top five factors and, in fact, showed up fairly low in the list selected by an average of 55 percent of respondents. However, a different picture emerges when we look at the data for firms that were outgrowing their peers in their industry sector, illustrated by the orange dots. For those winning companies, social impact was tied with talent management as the second in their list of critical factors enabling growth, following data and analytics. Notice also the gap between the winning companies and the lagging companies shaded in grey. The gap is similar in most areas but greatest in social impact. For managers in the lagging companies, social impact was the least important factor.

Managers in the winning companies in our sample were not relegating social impact to someone else. They were internalizing it and seeing it as one more lever to help them compete in the marketplace. While managers in lagging companies were thinking of social impact as a distraction, managers in winning companies were embracing what social impact can represent to their growth, what it can mean to their innovation, or their ability to serve new markets.

The conclusion from the research is in sharp contrast to the perception of many managers. Social impact benefits are strongly associated with firm performance. However, that association varies across industries, brand types, and customer segments. Therefore, it escapes the simplicity of binary frames like distraction or necessity. In fact, it can be both. If social impact is embedded into product offerings for categories where it does not matter or for customers who do not consider it, then, it can translate into a distraction or a misallocation of resources that could have been better used in other activities. However, a similar misallocation can occur if managers ignore social impact in product categories or customer segments, which is becoming a critical decision driver of purchase. Therefore, the key is for managers to avoid thinking of social impact in binary terms and instead apply the same strategic thinking and innovation they consistently use for other growth investments. This creates the need for a social impact strategy.

In the chapters that follow, we address each of these barriers by showing how managers can overcome the forces that contribute to inertia and instead find good growth.

Notes

1 Nielsen (2022). Nielsen's inaugural brand sustainability report reveals Australian consumer perceptions of the sustainability efforts of leading brands.

Chapter 4

Creating a Social Impact Strategy

Integrating sustainability and ESG goals into your business is a necessary condition for competing today. Few businesses can thrive without an active agenda that seeks to reduce or transform their environmental or social impact. Yet, it is important to recognize that those investments can happen in three different areas of an organization. The supply side of a business and how it impacts the environment or the community is a necessary effort by many investors and stakeholders today. As discussed earlier, the goals of that investment tend to be focused on cost reduction, risk reduction, or regulatory compliance. A second way sustainability investments connect to a business is through the way leaders attract, manage, and engage talent. Many companies have initiatives to help employees contribute to their communities in direct or indirect ways via donations or participation in volunteering events. For instance, Home Depot has a very active program where employees volunteer to build or repair neighborhood parks or homes. The goals of these initiatives center around employee retention, corporate reputation, and community engagement.

However, it is important to notice that despite the value of the supply and employee sides of social impact initiatives, they are not always well suited to play a role in the demand side of your business. When integrating social impact benefits into your product offerings and the customer experience, the goals are different from those in the supply or employee side, and therefore, the strategies may need to vary. Most importantly, while investing in the sustainability of your supply chain or employee engagement is a requirement for a business in many cases, integrating social impact into your value proposition is not. It is a strategic choice that, if done right, can provide you with a significant competitive advantage but, if not, can lead to distractions. This is why it is so important to start with a robust social impact strategy. To do so, managers must first identify the size of the social impact market in their industry or product category to determine if it is worth the investment. If they find sufficient market demand for social impact benefits, the strategy process begins by seeking answers to three questions—which societal need area to focus on, what contribution to make, and what return to expect.

DOI: 10.4324/9781003383246-5

You might be familiar with Brita, the water filter brand owned by The Clorox Company. What you may not know is the role that a social impact strategy had on their business. It's a remarkable example of taking a simple, straightforward product and connecting it to an environmental need, thus unlocking a significant amount of good growth. But let's take a step back and review where they came from in order to better appreciate the value of their social impact strategy.

Figure 4.1 is an example of one of the original labels used by the brand early in its entry into the United States market. Notice the type of benefits used to promote the product. First, there was a focus on functional benefits—Brita provided a way to get cleaner water from your faucet. The ad goes into detail about the efficacy of the product and the chemicals it eliminates. Finally, it signals its competition—tap water—by defining itself as a faucet mount system of water filtration. These claims tell us a lot about their growth strategy. It suggests that their intent for growth comes from converting tap water drinkers into filtered water drinkers which leads to their value proposition—cleaner tap water. It is also important to note that the product was a faucet filter, which meant that its growth would come

Figure 4.1 Brita marketing material showcasing early emphasis on water quality and functionality.

from water consumption at home. This is a critical consideration because we consume water on many occasions. However, their positioning focused only on one of those occasions and one of those locations, constraining their growth opportunity to drink water used at home. Fast forward a few years and a new growth strategy emerged, which could be seen through their actions in the marketplace. There was a product shift from the faucet filter to the water pitcher. This innovation gave them more flexibility to compete in more water consumption moments. It still serves a purpose in the kitchen, but it is no longer limited by the type of faucet a person uses. Importantly, the pitcher also means the product can be used in more locations where a faucet may not be available such as an office, a school dorm, or even a bedroom. Still, a more subtle and material change in strategy was also in place—a change in their source of growth. Remember that from its inception, Brita's source of growth was mainly focused on taking market share from tap water users and usage, essentially converting tap water users into filtered water users. A review of water consumption in the United States at the time shows that close to 70 percent of water drinking occurred at home and 30 percent outside of the house[1]. That meant that Brita was not participating in a significant portion of the market. Importantly, people's adoption of bottled water was accelerating and accounted for 38 percent of all water consumption, almost matching the amount of tap water consumption at home. Considering the fact that, on average, Americans pay 1 cent for 5 gallons of tap water, and the average price of 20 ounces of bottled water is $1.50, the revenue size of the bottled water market is significantly more attractive. However, how do we compete against bottled water with its elaborate branding, large marketing budgets, and variety of claims? Also, which segment of the bottled water market should the company focus on? The high-end, mid-tier, or lower-price segments?

To find an answer, they first needed to identify an unmet need and a benefit edge. Despite the difference in price, design, and water claims, all bottled water brands had the same limitation—using plastic as their primary packaging material. Awareness of plastic pollution was growing due to increasing media coverage, documentary films, and consumer stories on social media. Plastic pollution seemed like an emerging need the brand could address. Their role would be to provide an alternative to plastic without sacrificing water quality. Moreover, their mission became clear—great taste with less waste. However, they could not compete with the convenience of bottled water by only offering a faucet filter or a jar. Product innovation was needed to deliver that new value proposition. It came in the form of a bottle with Brita filter technology embedded in it. With their new value proposition, they could aim to grow from both the "at home" and "away from home" consumption occasions and capture share from both tap water and bottled water drinkers. As evidenced by the ads in Figure 4.2, their communication shifted from a functional benefit to a societal benefit (i.e. less plastic pollution). And it worked. Brita experienced a growth of 40 percent during the first few years of the new strategy and, by 2015, commanded a 70 percent market share[2]. Still today, they have continued this value proposition, and despite introducing new designs and faster filtration, Brita sustained their focus on the environmental benefits of their product. There is another aspect to consider regarding this change in strategy: the use of a societal benefit to drive growth. What can the bottled water competitors do in response to Brita's actions? Imagine that you work for Dasani, Aquafina, or one of the other bottled water brands and started to see Brita's growth coming in part from consumption of your category. What actions could you take to stop Brita and protect your share of the market? If your competitor was another brand of bottled water, you could innovate your product, look for differentiating package designs, or even consider price promotions. But in this case, the competitor is growing by attacking a feature of your product that you cannot change, at least in the short term—your packaging material. Bottled water brands do not have an easy alternative and economically viable alternative to plastic. Hence, it will take them years to develop a packaging design that can provide similar benefits but also protect their operating margins. Therefore, the Brita move is an example of a new entry into a category with a value proposition that the incumbents cannot replicate and is also attractive enough to take market share from them. That is precisely the behavior that economists and strategy researchers call "disruptive innovation."

In Brita, we have an example of a brand that used social impact to disrupt a new market and in doing so, found good growth that created a societal and a commercial benefit simultaneously. Their venture into bottled water contributed to a broader change in market dynamics and created the conditions for the subsequent success of plastic-busters like the Stanley drinking cups.

Figure 4.2 Examples of Brita's marketing material illustrating their environmental benefit vs. bottled water.

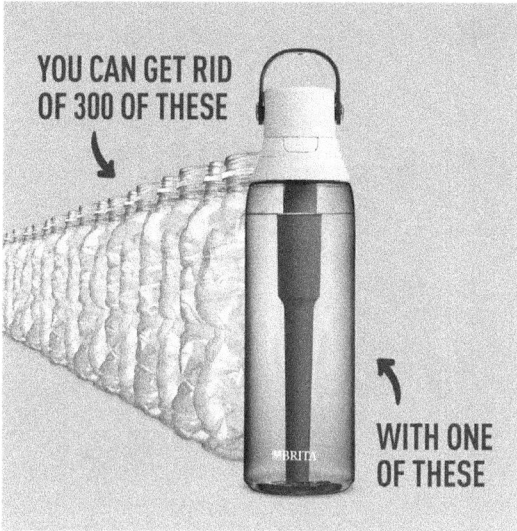

The Brita case illustrates the components of an effective social impact strategy. Before the messages and marketing campaigns were introduced, the Brita team made three critical choices. First, there was the choice of a societal need. In their case, it centered on an environmental issue, particularly plastic waste. Second, it is important to acknowledge that the plastic waste problem has many different causes. These include the use of plastic, the inefficiency in post-consumption collection, the economics of the recycling industry, and the behavior of consumers, among others. They chose a specific cause to focus on: the use of plastic in the consumption of water. Finally, they selected a specific mission: to replace plastic bottles with Brita. In retrospect, these choices seem to make sense and may even feel obvious. However, when managers are sitting at the start of the social impact journey, without clarity on the societal need or the mission, the process of crafting a social impact strategy can seem daunting and risky. In this next section, we will break down the formation of the social impact strategy into three components and provide guidance on how to implement them in different situations.

Notes

1 U.S. Department of Agriculture, Agricultural Research Service (2008). *Water: Beverage and moisture intakes 2005–2006* (Dietary Data Brief No. 7).
2 Fehrenbacher, K. (2015, April 15). Can this startup end Brita's water market dominance with a more beautiful filter?. *Fast Company*.

Chapter 5

Define a Societal Need

There are many societal needs that a business can be involved in. You can broadly separate the options between environmental issues and social issues. Even within that, there is a long list of potential areas. The question is, which one should you focus on? There are numerous sustainability actions that a company might take when managing its operations or motivating its employees. You may have programs to reduce energy waste or improve water use in the manufacturing process. Or you may be working to improve equity and inclusion in your organization. Companies increasingly have formal ESG reports with goals, plans, and programs that address a vast array of sustainability areas. While they all make sense as part of a general enterprise agenda, they may not be relevant to your customers.

We conceptualize the choice of a social impact area as a pyramid, with the bottom being the large number of societal issues that a brand simply cannot address and will choose to exclude. It is important to know your boundaries when it comes to social impact so you can focus resources and avoid involvement in areas that, while important, may not be suitable for your brand. Then, there are societal issues which you will address in your business practices such as the adoption of renewable energy by Budweiser or DEI practices to guide your employee hiring and promotion. These are foundational actions that respond to a company's ESG or sustainability agenda but might not be well suited for a role in the customer experience. Then, there are societal benefits that you could claim for regulatory or competitive reasons like the use of recycled plastic in your packaging. It is not a benefit you decide to compete on but a feature of your product. Lastly, there is a societal need that you might focus your brand's actions on, which becomes central to your value proposition and your competitive positioning.

Consider the example of Dove, a beauty product brand that is one of the most discussed and celebrated cases of social impact in business.

If we apply the pyramid framework to the case of Dove, we start by clarifying the boundaries. In other words, the areas where they will not act are located at the bottom of the pyramid. For instance, they don't have a formal program for animal rights protection in the testing of products.

DOI: 10.4324/9781003383246-6

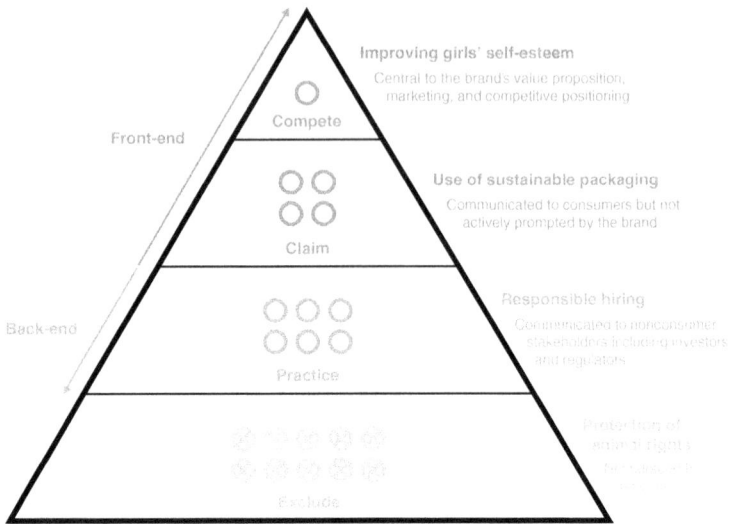

From "Competing on Social Purpose," September—October 2017,
By Omar Rodríguez Vilá and Sundar Bharadwaj

Figure 5.1 A Closer Look: The Dove Brand.

Moving up from there, there are a number of societal areas that Unilever as a company is involved in but are not part of the brand's value proposition to customers. Examples include responsible hiring and sustainable agriculture, particularly for the procurement of palm oil. Then, we move to the top of the pyramid to identify the one societal need area they do compete on—improving girls' self-esteem. That was a choice made in connection to their brand positioning and an area they wanted to be known for. The pyramid structure of the framework is important not only to clarify boundaries, but also to indicate that while there are numerous societal actions that a firm might take, there should be few, and ideally one, areas that form the basis of how you compete on social impact. For Allbirds, it is carbon reduction; for Dove, it is girls' self-esteem; for Always, it is women's empowerment; for Chipotle, it is sustainable agriculture; for Patagonia, it is environmental protection, etc… Therefore, the first step of the social impact strategy is about answering one question: What is that one societal benefit you're going to compete on?

Many companies have established methods for prioritizing their sustainability agenda. One of the most commonly accepted approaches supported by the Global Reporting Initiative and the Sustainability Accounting Standards Board is the materiality analysis. The concept of materiality is well established in finance and is an important criterion for selecting information suited for investor disclosures. It is based on the premise of relevance and the fact that information about a firm is only useful to the reader if it is material to financial decisions. In March of 1999, the Global Reporting Initiative published its first draft of the Sustainability Reporting Guidelines. In it, they proposed the adoption of materiality for the selection of information and priorities related to sustainability. The materiality analysis was derived from the guidelines as a tool to guide the formation of ESG goals and plans. Firms use it to evaluate the importance of different sustainability needs to their business operations and to their stakeholders, mainly regulators, employees, and investors. The result is a scatterplot matrix that illustrates the most critical sustainability areas for a given company, thus shaping the formation of its ESG agenda. For instance, consider the Sustainability report by Unilever, the Dutch-based multinational company behind global brands like Dove, Axe, and Seventh Generation. Conducted in 2021, their materiality assessment identified a total of 125 topics organized around 13 areas. They then evaluated the importance of each topic across different stakeholders, including retail customers, consumers, non-commercial stakeholders like regulators or NGOs, and suppliers. The result was a prioritized list of sustainability topics which shape the ESG agenda and actions that will impact the operations of the business.

Take agricultural sourcing or water usage; both have high importance among stakeholders and a significant impact on their business. When you look through their sustainability report, you're going to see initiatives to

Figure 5.2 Example of materiality analysis at Unilever.

improve their practices around ingredient sourcing and water usage. However, the prevention and treatment of communicable diseases or the protection of the marine environment are much lower on the assessment of materiality and, hence, are topics likely to be excluded from their ESG agenda. This is an analysis used at the formation of a sustainability strategy to identify priorities at a firm level. Companies will choose those areas that matter most, which means they are important to a business and core to the stakeholders. This is an especially useful, insightful, and practical approach to determining the ESG goals of a company.

However, it is a limited approach if you are trying to decide how to compete on social impact. The main shortcoming is that the framework does not reflect the specific needs of customers, nor the effect that a particular social impact area would have on customers' decisions about a firm's products or services. In that sense, the materiality analysis is not a customer or market-facing framework. Your ability to understand what matters to customers is reduced and impaired. And it's not necessarily the case that if you pick the upper right-hand quadrant, it will translate into a societal benefit for your customers in a way that will help you win in the marketplace. The materiality analysis represents a good place to start because it gives you an initial choice set where the firm is already actively involved. However, it is not the correct framework to guide the market-facing social impact choice. A more meaningful framework guiding the demand-side choices for societal benefits is one that contrasts brand fit with customer value. We call it the Brand Fit Assessment.

Brand Fit Assessment

Chris Kempczinski is currently the CEO of McDonald's and was leading the company during the phase of social unrest that emerged in the United States following claims of election fraud. In an interview with The New York Times in 2021, he was asked about his position on company activism, particularly the decision by McDonald's to stay silent on issues of voting rights in the United States. His answer provides insights into the meaning and importance of brand fit:

> One of the things that I've had to think about is, where do we speak up on an issue, and where do we not speak up. The way we've looked at it is: Is it either directly in our industry, or does it go specifically to the pillars that we've said are going to matter to us? So we've talked about jobs and opportunities. We've talked about helping communities in crisis. We've talked about the planet. And we've talked about supporting local farmers and ranchers. Those are the areas that we've said are specific to our business where we feel like we've got a role to play. In the case of voting rights, it wasn't our business. It wasn't aligned with one of our leadership platforms. And we didn't feel like our voice was going to be particularly helpful in addressing the issue.

Kempczinski's comments illustrate the importance of being clear about the "fit" or alignment between a brand's capabilities, its perception, and the societal need. The number of societal issues that a brand could address often exceeds what is possible or desirable. Therefore, seeking a good fit between the brand and the selected need is a necessary step to focus the business's social-impact investments and also helps explain a lack of action in other areas.

Brand-cause fit is the most studied factor in the academic literature on cause-related marketing (Rita and Trigueros, 2016)[1]. Research has found that fit and the cognitive fluency it creates among a stakeholder audience are strongly associated with the success of a social impact strategy. There are conditions that may alter the effect of fit, but when looking for a decision criterion to narrow down the plethora of social impact options for a brand, brand-cause fit is a critical place to start.

But what is "fit"? How do you know when you have it? Scholars define it as the perceived congruence between a social impact area and the brand. In other words, does it "make sense" for a brand to be actively seeking to support a specific societal need? (Lafferty, Goldsmith, and Hult, 2004[2]; Lafferty and Edmondson, 2009[3]). A "good fit" is measured by the extent to which consumers perceive the support to be logical, complementary, and congruent (Rigo et al., 2020[4]; Bigné-Alcañizetal, 2012[5]; Steckstor, 2011[6]). Research studies find that brand-cause fit moderates the effect of social impact messages and programs on consumer attitudes and choices toward a brand. (Hou, Du, and Li, 2008[7]; Nan and Heo, 2007[8]). This means higher brand-cause fit is associated with greater consumer response to a social impact program.

Going back to the examples we reviewed in Chapter 1, think about the extent to which it made sense for beer drinkers that Budweiser advertises their adoption of renewable energy when brewing the product. The use of wind or solar energy is an important step in the reduction of carbon emissions. It is undoubtedly a critical, admirable, and important supply chain innovation. However, its role in the demand chain is less obvious, and the conceptual fit between Budweiser's brand meaning and wind-powered energy is not as clear as Budweiser's fit with, say, baseball or national holiday celebrations like July 4. Alternatively, consider the relationship between Chipotle and sustainable agricultural practices. This is also a supply chain innovation, but in this case, it creates value on the demand side as well by differentiating the product in relevant ways. Importantly, because sustainable agriculture has been a part of Chipotle's value proposition from its early days, it is part of its meaning. Therefore, their demand-side actions related to organic ingredients or fair trade are perceived with a high degree of fit among consumers, strengthening their ability to turn social impact investments into growth.

Brand-cause fit comes from a match between the brand associations and the social impact area. To understand a brand's associations, simply ask yourself, what is your brand "known for"? Importantly, do not answer that question from your perspective, and be careful not to answer it with a list of associations you aspire to have. The only associations that matter are those that stakeholders have, in particular, customers. Therefore, investigate the associations that customers have with a brand. It is also important to note that a brand's associations can come from two sources. First, the degree of fit can be derived from a brand's association with specific functional features or competencies—areas where a brand is uniquely able to contribute, owing to its perceived capabilities or functionality. For instance, as we will discuss later in the book, SunTrust Bank leveraged its competencies to launch a successful social-impact program around financial security, education, and tools in communities where it does business, strengthening employee engagement and building customer loyalty. Similarly, Nike's effort to expand the participation of women in sports was consistent with their products and business.

However, the known features or competencies of a product are not the only source of fit. Another option for managers to find a cause fit is to understand the brand's associations. There are images or emotional traits built by the brand over its history through advertising messages or actions taken in the market. For instance, there is no inherent functional association between polar bears and soft drinks. There is no competency fit between the functionalities or capabilities of soft drink companies and the work to protect the Arctic environment that supports their livelihood. Unless your brand is Coca-Cola, which, has used polar bear imagery in their advertising since the 1930s. Those associations supported a high-fit partnership with the World Wildlife Federation to develop a new refuge for polar bears. We will discuss this case in great detail in a later chapter. In contrast, the brand Pepsi had no historical association with issues of racial justice or civil rights. That lack of fit contributed to the negative response it received from consumers when it tried to attach the brand to the Black Lives Matter movement in an ad featuring Kendall Jenner.

Therefore, the social impact strategy starts with knowing your brand well and having clarity about the specific features, competencies, or image-based associations that customers perceive the brand to have. Those associations become the first clue in finding the right societal need space. After evaluating areas of high fit between your brand and different societal needs, consider the importance or relevance of those societal needs to your customers. As discussed later, pay particular attention to the design of the research studies and methodologies used in assessing the importance of social impact on your customers or audience of interest. Using methods that do not account for social desirability bias can lead to vast oversizing of the opportunity. Contrasting customer utility with brand-cause fit for each societal need area will generate a new plot to guide decisions about the potential area of focus for your brand.

Consider the case of Cinnabon, a retail chain selling baked goods. The marketing team was compelled to explore the role of social impact on their business, but they were not clear how their brand, known for indulgence, could authentically support a societal need. To generate an initial list of potential societal need areas, we conducted a simple exercise that helped them identify possible associations across both functional and image dimensions by answering a simple question: "What is Cinnabon known for among _____?". We changed the stakeholder group to get to a broader list of potential areas. What is Cinnabon known for older customers? Younger customers? Infrequent customers? Regular customers? Importantly, we involved people with different lenses in the business, not only marketing managers but also operation managers and store managers. The exploration led to a list of surprising potential associations. There were the expected associations with taste, their best-selling products, and their shopping mall location. But other associations also came up, including the fact that Cinnabon was known as the first job of many high school students in the communities they served. In the next step, we matched their associations to potential societal need areas coming from the 17 UN Sustainable Development Goals. Alternatively, the firm's ESG or sustainability agenda can be used in this step, but you should not limit your list to items in the sustainability report. The reason, as discussed earlier, is that the ESG agenda is rarely driven by demand-side considerations since they tend to be based on supply chain risks, regulatory conditions, or employee expectations. Therefore, make sure you bring a broader set of potential societal need areas to the table than those that your company is already working on.

Mapping the associations with the societal need areas helped generate a list of 20 potential societal need areas. In addition to fit, managers must also factor in customer utility—how important addressing a given issue is to the brand's customers. We then conducted a study with their relevant customer groups to assess conceptual fit and importance. Basically, we asked customers of Cinnabon what extent each of the 20 areas made sense for Cinnabon to support, and how important those societal needs were to them. Our team used the data to generate a brand-fit assessment, a simple yet insightful tool to help brands narrow their choice of societal needs. Figure 5.3 shows the resulting map and the cluster of highest-fit/highest-utility societal needs in the upper right quadrant.

The findings from the study were revealing to the management team. While much of the industry discussion was focused on the environmental footprint of food service restaurants, that was not an area their customers associated strongly with Cinnabon. However, many customers associated Cinnabon with job creation in their community, and in particular, the first job that many had during high school. In addition, a large percentage also found that area of impact to be important to them. The combination of customer utility and fit helped them narrow down the potential list of social impact areas to the role they played in enabling young people to transition into the workplace.

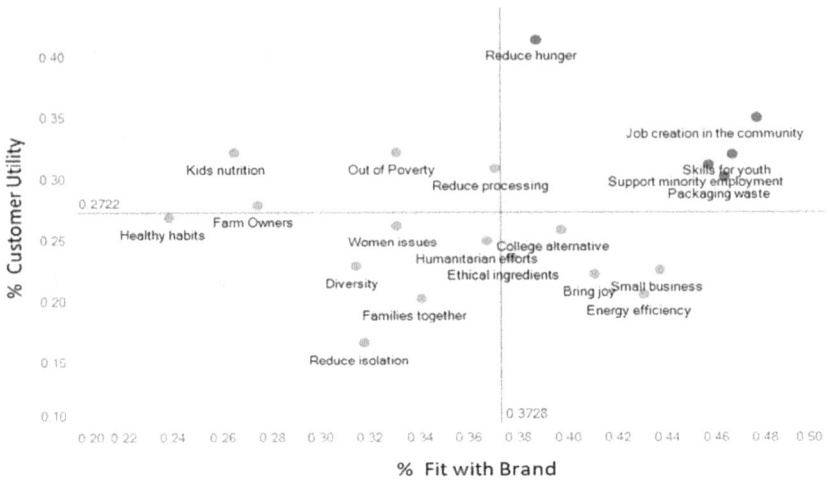

Figure 5.3 Analysis to inform the selection of a societal need by contrasting brand fit with customer utility for each societal need area.

There is one important exception to the importance of brand-cause fit on the effect of social impact programs. When the societal need area has high levels of awareness and importance among a large share of the population, the importance of fit in influencing consumer response decreases (Zdravkovic et al., 2010)[9]. It seems that consumers care more about a brand contributing to an issue that matters to them than if the issue per se is related to the brand's product.

To ensure a robust brand-fit assessment, managers need to generate a comprehensive list of potential social impact areas, which can be a daunting task. As discussed earlier, start with the societal needs present in the firm's ESG or sustainability report. Then, societal need areas will be added based on the brand associations or known competencies. Finally, it is also important to include topics related to the positive or negative externalities of your brand. This means that societal need areas are those in which your brand is already contributing to or impacting in its normal course of action. For instance, for bottled water brands, it can be plastic or water access. For food service restaurants, it can be sustainable agriculture or food waste. In their Journal of Marketing study, Nickerson et al. found a significant difference in the effect of social impact programs based on their relationship to product externality. The authors categorize social impact efforts as corrective, compensatory, or cultivating. Corrective actions were actions directly seeking to reduce a negative externality of a product or service. For instance, Evian's launch of a bottle made from aluminum material is an action seeking to directly reduce the effect of plastic pollution by their product. Compensatory actions relate to the negative externality but do not directly change the brand activities. One example is when a bottled water brand invests in promoting recycling programs. The investment is not about changing their direct contribution to the problem, but instead on related efforts that seek to address it. Finally, cultivating actions refer to social impact efforts unrelated to the negative externalities of the brand such as when a bottled water brand invests in promoting women's empowerment.

The researchers built a dataset of 80 CSR initiatives across 55 brands and measured the influence of the three types of announcements on brand sales. They found a material difference in the sales effect based on the type of social impact program. Those related to a brand externality, either by correcting or compensating, were found to have a positive and significant effect on sales. Those they categorized as cultivating had, in fact, a negative effect on product sales. The findings suggest that it might be best to focus on societal needs that have a direct or indirect link to your product. It is not enough to "do good"—you need to create societal benefits in areas that are related to your product offering or brand. As a result, corrective actions designed to reduce or eliminate a negative externality are a good place to start. Compensatory actions, those designed to augment a positive externality—a social or environmental contribution that emerges naturally from your product functionality or brand heritage - can also become valuable areas to consider. Between the ESG agenda and the potential compensatory or corrective actions of a brand, managers should be able to generate a valuable list of potential alternatives for social impact.

The Vaseline Healing Project

Let's work through an example exploring the design of a social impact strategy by Vaseline intensive care lotion, a staple product in many homes. Before we describe the story of their social impact work, it might be worthwhile to do a quick mental exercise and consider what possible social impact areas could be for the Vaseline brand. Should they focus on environmental issues and adopt recycled packaging or environmentally friendly packaging? Should they consider social causes more related to the product? Here is the first moment to apply the insight we discussed earlier; start by thinking about what Vaseline is already known for as a product and brand.

The Vaseline marketing team, led by Kathleen Dunlop, was charged by then CEO Paul Polman to add a social impact dimension to the brand. This was all part of a broader firm effort to extend the number of brands with a social purpose in their portfolio. Katheleen and her team created a task force including internal and external partners, particularly agency partners, to think through different options for social impact programs. They explored several areas but had no clear path for the workshops. Initially, it was difficult to envision a social impact strategy that made sense for a type of product, that was so functional in nature. Also, Vaseline did not have the cultural influence of brands like Nike or Coca-Cola. But then again, neither did Dove when it started, and that gave them confidence that they might be able to find the right societal need on which to ground their strategy. They continued to explore potential societal need areas, but this time, they gave the team an assignment to identify ways by which Vaseline was already having a positive impact on society. In the weeks following their last workshop, one team member came across a news article in the Washington Post about the refugee crisis in the Southern part of Europe[10]. The article, entitled "*What can a dermatologist do in a Syrian refugee camp?*" was written by Dr. Grace Bandow and Dr. Samer Jaber, two dermatologists who responded to a request by Dr. Humam Akbik to join a medical mission to Jordan. Their story provided an overview of the dire conditions faced by refugees from the political and military crisis that impacted Syria in the 2010s. It shared some of the serious health risks that even minor cuts to the skin could introduce, owing to unsanitary living conditions and the potential for the spread of infections. Included in the article was an image of the first aid kit used by dermatologists to care for the skin conditions of people at the refugee camps. In the kit, there was a small jar of Vaseline. "We prepared for a parasitic infection called leishmaniasis, which causes skin lesions. We brought medicine for bacterial skin infections like impetigo. But it never occurred to us to prioritize Vaseline petroleum jelly as an item of high importance when we packed our supplies for the Syrian refugee camps," wrote Dr. Bandow and Dr. Jaber. They later explained how Vaseline became their first line of defense against skin infections and one of the main weapons to protect people in these environments.

A light bulb went off in the manager's mind—the social impact they were trying to figure out was already happening. Doctors are using the product to serve a critical societal need, and Vaseline managers do not even know about it. Kathleen reached out to the Direct Relief organization and contacted Dr. Bandow and Dr. Jaber, inviting them for a meeting to discuss their needs and ways in which the brand could help. The subsequent meetings with the doctors led to the formation of a program called the Vaseline Healing Project, with a mission to ensure that Vaseline was never missing from the refugee camps in Europe. However, they quickly realized the need for Vaseline in distressed conditions was unfortunately not limited to these refugee camps. There were many situations around the world that put people in conditions of physical distress where Vaseline could help. Therefore, their vision quickly expanded and now states, "*The Vaseline® Healing Project provides dermatological care, Vaseline® Jelly, and medical supplies needed to help restore the skin of people affected by poverty or emergencies around the world.*" Their mission became to make Vaseline accessible and available in places where people are experiencing conditions of distress that impose a substantial risk to their well-being. These could be displacement resulting from weather events like hurricanes or tornados or political con-flict like in the case of Syria. The program eventually expanded to cover all 50 states in the United States and over 70 countries worldwide.

This is an example of a brand that went through a process and eventually found a social impact area that was right for them, not only because it helped them build on the sustainability agenda of Unilever and contribute in a material way to an important societal need, but also because it helped them win in the marketplace.

To create the Vaseline Healing Project, the team had to convince the business unit managers of different countries, including South Africa and the United States, two of their leading markets, to allocate funds that would otherwise be used in programs to grow the business. In essence, they needed to go beyond a moral case about the potential to do "good" and help busi-ness leaders with pressures deliver their revenue and profit numbers and envision how the project could advance their objectives.

We will describe their methods in subsequent chapters, but for now, it is important to focus on how they found clarity on their societal need area. Instead of asking, "What societal impact benefit can we create?", they asked a different question—how is Vaseline already creating a positive social impact? In trying to answer that question, they uncover the most effective social impact benefit for their brand - one that fit with their pro-duct benefits and heritage, and also touched upon areas important to cus-tomers, particularly as the program expanded to support local communities. Perhaps if they had looked solely at societal needs without considering the product externalities, they might have concluded that there were no clear societal needs for the brand to support or would have simply adopted an area already present in the company's ESG agenda. Seeing new opportunities can change the question.

It is important to also realize that the societal need to protect people's well-being in moments of distress was not present in Unilever's materi-ality analysis at the time. This chapter outlined the starting point for crafting a social impact strategy—making a choice about a societal need area. To do so, it is important to keep in mind the following con-siderations—do not limit the list to the sustainability agenda of your firm. Generate an expanded list of potential social impact areas by con-sidering your product externalities and brand associations. Finally, ask the question, "Where or how are we currently having a positive societal impact?"—as it might help uncover a need area that is already being served by your product. After generating a list of options, select an area where your brand has fit. Then, move to the second step of the social impact strategy process, the decision about how to contribute to that societal need in a way that is meaningful and material. That is what we call selecting your brand's societal mission.

Notes

1 Guerreiro, J., Rita, P., & Trigueiros, D. (2016). A Text Mining-Based Review of Cause-Related Marketing Literature. *Journal of Business Ethics, 139*(1), 111–128.
2 Lafferty, B. A., Goldsmith, R. E., & Hult, G. T. M. (2004). The impact of the alliance on the partners: A look at cause–brand alliances. *Psychology & Marketing, 21*(7), 509–531.
3 Lafferty, B. A. & Edmondson, D. R. (2009). Portraying the cause instead of the brand in cause-related marketing ads: Does it really matter?. *Journal of Marketing Theory and Practice, 17*(2), 129–144.
4 Rigo, G. M., Braga, S. S., & Silva, D. S. (2020). Cause-related marketing: A trade-off between marketers and consumers. *Independent Journal of Management & Production, 11*(8), 2411–2430.
5 Bigné-Alcañiz, E., Currás-Pérez, R., Ruiz-Mafé, C., & Sanz-Blas, S. (2012). Cause-related marketing influence on consumer responses: The moderating effect of cause–brand fit. *Journal of Marketing Communications, 18*(4), 265–283.
6 Steckstor, D. (2011). The effects of cause-related marketing on customers' attitudes and buying behavior. *Business Research, 4*(2), 198–218.
7 Hou, J., Du, L., & Li, J. (2008). Cause's attributes influencing consumer's purchasing intention: Empirical evidence from China. *Asia Pacific Journal of Marketing and Logistics, 20*(4), 363–380.
8 Nan, X. & Heo, K. (2007). Consumer responses to corporate social responsibility (CSR) initiatives: Examining the role of brand–cause fit in cause-related marketing. *Journal of Advertising, 36*(2), 63–74.
9 Zdravkovic, S., Magnusson, P., & Stanley, S. M. (2010). Dimensions of fit between a brand and a social cause and their influence on attitudes. *International Journal of Research in Marketing, 27*(2), 151–160.
10 Murphy, M. (2014, June 23). Here's what Syrian doctors need most: Vaseline. *The Washington Post.*

Chapter 6

Selecting the Brand Societal Mission

To determine the right social impact strategy for a brand, it is not sufficient to find a societal need with good brand fit and customer relevance. After taking that step, managers need to decide the specific contribution their brand can make to that societal need—what we call the *Brand Societal Mission*. Think of the Vaseline example we reviewed in the last chapter. Kathleen Dunlop and her team identified a societal need related to the well-being of people in conditions of distress. It started with refugee camps in Europe, but the need was broader given that, unfortunately, people face similar conditions of displacement and distress all too often for both political and environmental reasons. In this second step of the social impact strategy process, managers need to answer an important question—what role could their brand play? In the case of Vaseline, what mission could they serve within the societal need? What is their unique role and contribution to the situation, considering all the other organizations and efforts involved in alleviating the problem? Clarity on the *Brand Societal Mission* will guide the formation of programs, partners, and allocation of resources. Societal needs such as expanding education, reducing climate change, or mitigating hunger are vast and complex problems, typically exacerbated by numerous interrelated propagating factors. With many organizations already involved, finding a useful and specific role for a brand to play requires a significant effort. One technique that can help managers clarify their societal mission is the root cause analysis. It can help them see possible areas where contributions are needed and decide where their brand can play a real and material role.

In the case of Vaseline, there are many risks to the well-being of refugees, and if we narrow the assessment to their physical health as impacted by their skin conditions, we still have a number of potential root causes of concern. Poor hygiene, limited hydration, exposure to extreme heat, low nutrition, and difficult access to knowledge or treatments are just a few of the factors contributing to skin-related illnesses for people living in displaced and distressed conditions. The brand team must decide which of those potential root causes they are in the best position to impact. Where can they make the biggest difference? This is not a decision they made in

DOI: 10.4324/9781003383246-7

isolation. In fact, quite the opposite. They consulted with the medical team working directly in the refugee camps to understand the needs and specific area where Vaseline could make a valuable difference. Their decision was to focus on one of the root causes—access to skin care products. From there, their social impact mission became clear, and the programs followed.

After deciding on a societal need area, managers need to understand the different root causes contributing to that need in order to identify a specific and unique role for the brand. We worked with a juice brand in Brazil to help them through the process of crafting a societal mission. Managers had chosen malnourishment among children in underserved communities as their brand's societal need area of focus. They were worried about a decline in fruit consumption in families, particularly among those with children living in lower socioeconomic conditions. Still, malnourishment among children is a broad area of need, and to have a real impact, the team needed to be specific about which aspect of the problem they could seek to resolve or at least reduce. Malnourishment could be driven in part by a lack of access to nutritious foods, a negative perception of taste among children, a lack of affordability, constraints on parents' time when shopping for and preparing meals, or the absence of parents' education about the nutritional content of different foods, among others. It would be unproductive and unviable for a brand to address every factor that contributes to malnourishment, but by working on a single root cause, managers increase the odds that their social-impact investments can have a real effect on the issue. Considering their capabilities and product benefits, they focused on the educational aspect of the problem by providing parents with the information required for them to make better choices like nutritional elements or known risks associated with the product or its ingredients.

We also worked for a brand that sells workplace protection gear and construction footwear, including boots. They are well known as a high-quality brand among trade professionals and are seeking to add a societal benefit layer to their value proposition. After a series of studies, the brand team decided to focus on the social need of expanding access to trade education among youth as a way of increasing employment opportunities for people who decide that a college education is not the right path for them. Figure 6.1 shows a root-cause analysis we helped them create with a focus on youth unemployment and the need to fill employment gaps in trade professions.

The team developed the root cause map by reviewing existing research into the causes of youth unemployment and interviewing academics and thought leaders in that area. Significantly impacting that specific societal need would require action in one or more of the root causes. But by generating this map, the management team could better match the resources and capabilities of the brand to the areas of need. In this case, some areas, such as government policy or financial programs, were far removed from the brand's ability to make a difference. However, the team did find a role in the

Societal Need: Youth Unemployment

Lack of demand for workers due to macroeconomic conditions causes cyclical (demand-deficient) unemployment. Mismatch between worker skills/locations and employer needs causes structural unemployment. Inefficiencies involved in the transition between occupations causes frictional unemployment. Finally, education system has biased college education over technical schools, forcing some students into an educational path that is not best for them.

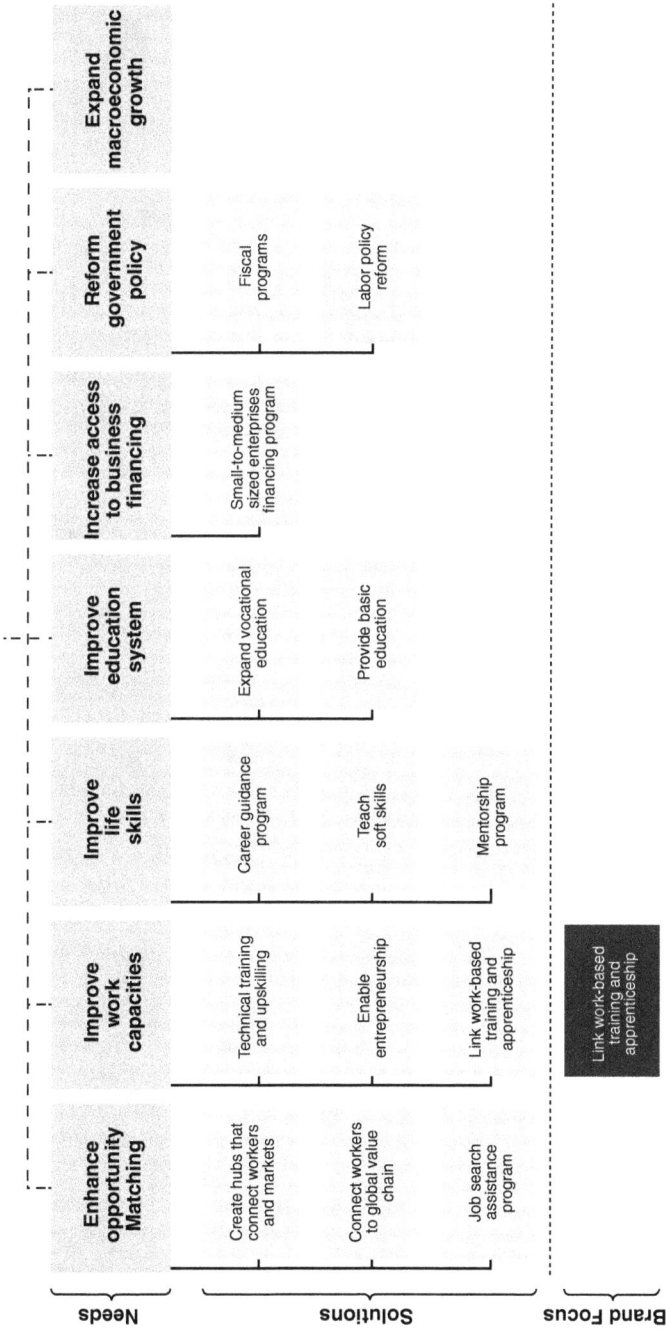

Needs

- Enhance opportunity Matching
- Improve work capacities
- Improve life skills
- Improve education system
- Increase access to business financing
- Reform government policy
- Expand macroeconomic growth

Solutions

- Enhance opportunity Matching: Create hubs that connect workers and markets; Connect workers to global value chain; Job search assistance program
- Improve work capacities: Technical training and upskilling; Enable entrepreneurship; Link work-based training and apprenticeship
- Improve life skills: Career guidance program; Teach soft skills; Mentorship program
- Improve education system: Expand vocational education; Provide basic education
- Increase access to business financing: Small-to-medium sized enterprises financing program
- Reform government policy: Fiscal programs; Labor policy reform

Brand Focus

- Link work-based training and apprenticeship

Figure 6.1 Societal Need: Youth Unemployment.

need to enhance opportunity matching, which means helping connect teens and young adults interested in trade jobs to the type of employment opportunities that their business system provided. That clarity of purpose enabled the brand to develop programs that ultimately contributed to the broader societal need in a way that was authentic and viable given their capabilities and heritage.

The root cause analysis, when informed by experts in the field, provides a rigorous roadmap for managers to identify the brand's societal mission, the second step in building a social impact strategy. Importantly, the root cause analysis should be conducted in close collaboration with organizations, either government or non-profits, which are actively working on the societal need area of choice. This is a critical difference between traditional marketing practices and competing on social impact—the need to partner effectively with non-commercial stakeholders. Establishing and managing partnerships is a common business activity, but as a leader of social impact work for a brand, managers will need to know how to partner with organizations that either lack a financial incentive or are not profit-driven. We will explore this critical capability in later chapters, but it is enough to say that competing on social impact requires skilled stakeholder management.

Once you have identified the root causes and specific areas your brand can contribute to, the last step is to clarify the approach you will take to create the societal benefit. In other words, what action will your brand take to achieve the societal mission? In our study of market interventions by over 70 brands, we identified five models that managers can use to answer this final question. Figure 6.2 describes each of the models, the associated managerial roles, and the key organizational capabilities needed.

The first area of potential social impact is "Generate Resources" for organizations working to address societal needs. Most often, this takes the form of donations by a brand based on a purchase and is executed via different tactics. One common practice in the retail or service industry is the round-up. At the moment of a transaction, the company asks if the customer would like to round up the cost and donate the additional portion to a particular charity. The ride-share company Lyft applied this tactic, as did the supermarket chain Publix, among many others. Regardless of the mechanism used, notice their societal impact comes in the form of generating resources to support a particular cause. Basically, the brand is supporting the fundraising efforts of non-profit organizations. Notice also that they are not involved in any specific action or intervention associated with the societal need. So, it is a low-touch, low-effort way of generating a societal benefit. Not surprisingly, owing to its ease of adoption, this is the most common model used by brands when trying to integrate a social benefit into their customer experience. Because it is so easy to adopt and so widely used, it is not very differentiating. However, it could be an effective way to start

	Generate Resources	Change Mindsets	Influence Behavior	Enhance Options	Improve Conditions
Definition	In this model the brand focuses on generating financial resources or facilitating access to talent, skills, or relationships for individuals or organizations working to serve the social need.	In this model the brand uses their advertising content or communication resources to influence the mindset of people around the social need in a direction that contributes to solving the social need.	In this model the brand focuses on changing the customer behavior in a direction that help address the social need.	In this model brands provide choices to consumers in the form of products or services that address a social need better than other alternatives in the market.	In this model brands seek to directly improve the conditions of an area affected by a social issue. In this case they become involved in development work, often in close collaboration with NGO partners.
Role	Managers are motivated by a need to demonstrate support for a societal need. The social impact is often tangential to the customer experience.	Managers are motivated by a market opportunity or consumer trend connected to their growth strategy. The social impact is central to the customer experience.	Managers are motivated by insights from life-cycle analysis or negative externalities of the product. The social impact is not present in the product offering.	Managers are motivated by a trend in consumer needs that relate directly to their products or services. The social impact is central to the product offering.	Managers are motivated by stakeholder pressures. The social impact is central to the customer experience.
Core Capability Needed	**Fundraising** Uses revenue generating activities to supply funds (or other resources) to organizations working to resolve the social issue. Requires NGO partnerships but not close collaboration.	**Storytelling** Use mainstream and often emotional communication in earlier stages of the consumer funnel to communicate their social benefits. Requires close collaboration with NGOs, Regulators and Sustainability teams.	**Nudging** Does not explicitly communicate the social benefits to users or consumers. Requires close collaboration with R&D and Sustainability teams.	**Activation** Uses mainstream product communication across the customer journey to communicate their social benefits. Requires close collaboration with R&D and Sustainability teams.	**Journalism** Uses highly targeted, often digital first and owned channels with longer form communications methods (e.g. documentaries, blogs) to communicate their social benefits. Requires close collaboration with NGOs, Regulators and Sustainability teams.
Example	The model used by the Newman's Own line of products to generate funds for the social issues they support.	Always, Dove, and Nike have adopted this job by seeking to change the social perspective on issues of women empowerment or diversity.	Cascade, P&G's line of dishwashing soap, identified the pre-washing of dishes as a large portion of their water footprint. Their impact focused on eliminating the need for pre-washing via product innovation.	Seventh Generation, Allbirds or Method which seeks to use their product innovation as a way of reducing the negative effects of cleaning products on the environment.	The Vaseline Healing project using their brand activities to improve the skin care provided to people in conditions of distress.

Figure 6.2 Description of social impact models.

embedding social impact into your brand, given its relatively simple execution and low levels of integration with the business operations. Importantly, this model can be executed in innovative ways, enhancing its ability to differentiate the offering. For instance, the insurtech startup Lemonade, a certified B Corporation, has disrupted a traditional industry by building a lovable brand utilizing social impact as an essential part of its mission and business model. Lemonade takes only 25 percent of its insurance premium from consumers to cover its administrative costs and profits. This percentage was well below the industry average. After accounting for claims, reinsurance, fees, and taxes, the firm gifted the unpaid claims to charities of the customers' choice instead of investing the rest. In the process, the firm upended the industry wherein the customers battled with the traditional industry firms for reimbursement, while firms benefited from not paying all the claims. In this win-lose battle, both sides raise accusations of dishonesty and mistrust. Lemonade, using a social impact approach and not claiming the unpaid claim float for itself, mitigated the mistrust and enhanced trust between the firm and the customers. The firm has donated over $10M to various charitable causes in less than a decade.

A second model frequently used is called "Changing Mindsets," where the brands take on the role of an advertiser for societal needs. This is a model of greater interdependency and resource commitment because brands allocate a portion of their communication investments, talent, and time to create content that can promote the societal cause or solutions to address societal needs. Take, for instance, Dove's decision to promote a healthier perception of beauty, which we will cover in greater depth in a later chapter. They were not offering to donate resources. Instead, they were investing resources to help change the cultural definition of beauty in a direction that would be more inclusive and supportive of girls. A similar approach was taken by Nike in what has become a classic example of social impact. In 1995 the then CEO, Phil Knight, decided to allocate some of its advertising resources not toward a new line of shoes, but rather towards the promotion of women in sports. The message, created by their agency Wieden & Kennedy, shared highlights of research about the impact of sports on the quality of life of women. It was not directed at girls but instead to their parents, coaches, and school officials in an effort to change the perception and increase the participation of girls in organized sports—helping them transition from fans to players. The ad hit a cultural nerve at the time, leading to a significant response of support. With it, Nike leaders were not making donations but rather changing mindsets, a different path for the creation of social impact. This strategy is best suited for companies that already have strong storytelling capabilities and a network of agencies and influencers that can help guide the creation of meaningful content.

Another example of changing mindsets is the campaign by Tata Tea in India. The brand's tagline was "Jaago Re," meaning "Wake up." Over a decade and a half, they leveraged this tagline in advertising for several societal issues, such as wake up to fight corruption, politician accountability, gender stereotyping, and violence against women. The brand emphasized how citizens have a responsibility to address these issues. Regarding gender stereotyping, they worked with India's Human Resources Ministry to create a curriculum included in schools. The campaign continues to be powerful and utilizes traditional television and social media to change consumers' perceptions of their role in social issues and government.

Always, the brand of female hygiene products, is another example of a brand that used this model effectively to create societal benefit. The brand launched a program in the United States to promote self-confidence among young girls. The organization was particularly concerned about gender bias and specific stereotypes that were limiting the belief of girls about their potential. "During puberty, young people become increasingly aware of what those around them think. When they're exposed to a society that consciously, or unconsciously, attributes certain attitudes or beliefs to specific genders, the effects can be limiting"—read one of the brand's statements. Their solution started with challenging the negative connotation that the phrase "Like a girl" often had in American culture, particularly in sports. Running "like a girl" or hitting "like a girl" was not celebrated but instead used as a phrase to describe someone who was underperforming. Similar to the Dove or Nike example, the campaign generated significant awareness of the societal need and stimulated many online conversations and exchanges. Yet, there lies its limitation. The "changing mindsets" model is tempting for marketers because it feels like familiar territory—executed via an advertising campaign, which, if done right, can generate significant attention for the brand and accolades for their creators. However, the actual contribution to the societal need is less clear. In the case of Dove, the effort was accompanied by a vast program to promote self-esteem education in schools by working with teachers and educators. It has also endured and is now celebrating almost 20 years since its inception.

Unfortunately, the holistic nature of the Dove social impact program is more of an exception than the norm among brands that opt for the "change mindsets" model. In most cases, the action is treated and budgeted as a campaign, frequently lasting one or two planning cycles. Furthermore, it can expose the brand to accusations of greenwashing, if the program is not accompanied by more tangible actions. However, if done in close partnership with other organizations providing services or solutions to address societal needs, the approach can play a critical role in expanding awareness among the public at large or specific stakeholder groups, which can then facilitate the effort of those more directly involved in the work.

A third model for creating social impact is "influencing behaviors." This model focuses on going beyond a change in mindset or way of thinking toward the adoption of new behaviors by customers in the marketplace. Importantly, the new behaviors should be in line with the chosen societal need. This is a model frequently adopted by consumer-packaged goods companies, in part because the environmental footprint of their products is often magnified by the way consumers actually use them. For instance, in a lifecycle analysis of toothpaste, shampoo, soap, or dishwasher products, most of the water usage will occur in consumers' homes, not in the manufacturing process. Consider Colgate, the brand of toothpaste, which created a campaign named "Every Drop Counts" that included a 60-second ad shown during the Super Bowl broadcast in an effort to promote a change in behavior by people when brushing their teeth—namely, to turn off the faucet.

The campaign had different messages and ran across multiple channels, but the goal was the same—to change user behavior that would lead to a lower environmental footprint.

Figure 6.3 Visual from Colgate's "Every Drop Counts" initiative promoting water conservation.

Procter and Gamble is applying the same model of social impact with its detergent brand, Tide. The campaign, "Cold Call," created by the advertising agency Saatchi & Saatchi, features American rap artist Tracy Lauren Marrow, also known as Ice-T, wrestler "Stone Cold" Steve Austin, and other celebrities calling consumers to ask them to consider washing their clothes with cold water.

The ads shared the lower cost, energy savings, and the related environmental benefits of switching to cold water wash. As expected, they also talk about a new Tide formulation specifically designed to work effectively with cold water. It is a fusion of societal and product benefits launched to coincide with Tide's 75th birthday and its Ambition 2030 announcement, which outlines Tide's key sustainability goals for the next decade.

The company used a similar model with its brand Cascade, a leading dishwasher detergent. The lifecycle analysis revealed that a significant amount of water waste occurred when people pre-washed dishes before putting them in the dishwasher.

Cascade's focus, particularly through its new formulations, was in part geared towards changing that behavior and encouraging consumers not to pre-wash their dishes. Notice that in all three examples, the brand goes beyond changing mindsets and intentionally works toward changing a behavior in the market—a behavior that if changed, would have a positive impact.

Building on an earlier example from Tata Tea's brand, a recent extension of their "Wake-up" campaign seeks to provoke a social movement and encourage citizens to pledge to recycle, save energy, and buy environmentally friendly

Figure 6.4 Tide's "Cold Call" campaign showcasing environmental benefits of washing clothes in cold water.

Figure 6.5 Example of Cascade's promotion to reduce the practice of pre-washing dishes prior to dishwasher use.

products, etc., thus extending to the domain of climate change and focusing on changing behaviors, not just opinions.

The fourth model for brand managers to consider is "Enhancing Options." In this case, the brand creates a product or service alternative that delivers a societal benefit, and therefore, social impact becomes central to the product offering. Marketing managers require close collaboration with the research, development, and sustainability teams to ensure the changes in the product translate into the desired social impact benefits. The Bona Wood floor cleaning products line is an example of a brand that uses this model. Through its different selection of offerings, the Bona company provides a viable and valuable alternative to floor replacement. Customers have the option to renovate their floors and then care for them in ways that significantly extend the life of the wood, eliminating or at least reducing the incidence of actual replacement and, hence, lowering the impact on the environment. The upgrades made by Autodesk to their building design software enabling engineers and architects to optimize energy consumption in their structural designs is another example of a brand creating social impact by enhancing the options available in the market. Boxed Water provides a differentiated option to consumers of bottled water by using carton packaging made primarily from renewable resources, eliminating the need for plastic. The line of cleaning products by Seventh Generation with lower levels of toxicity or the founders of Allbirds and their innovative manufacturing practices that created shoes with the lowest levels of CO_2 emissions are also examples of brands creating social impact by changing the nature of the alternatives available in the market. An interesting point to highlight is that in these cases, managers often cannot tell the difference between their traditional business and the social impact benefit. They are one and the same. They are not just competing on social impact, but simply competing in the market with a product they believe will help them win. That level of integration of social impact into the business model and growth agenda of a brand can, in fact, turn social impact into a competitive advantage, partly because it is harder to emulate by rivals.

As a result, it is also harder to implement and exit. Imagine what would happen if Allbirds stopped reporting and, more importantly, eliminated its efforts to reduce the carbon footprint from its manufacturing activities. In a way, it would no longer be the same brand. Therefore, while it offers one of the greatest potentials to create good growth, this model tends to be adopted more by newer brands than established ones. Older brands may find the transition to this type of societal benefit too expensive and risky to implement.

The last model for social impact is "Improve Conditions." In this case, the brand uses its resources to directly change one of the root causes of the societal need. Consider the example of the Vaseline Healing Project discussed earlier in the book. Their mission was to expand the availability of

Vaseline in refugee camps and other locations where skincare was of critical importance to the well-being of people in distress. They were not seeking to raise funds, change mindsets, change consumer behavior, or change the product. Instead, their mission was to improve the conditions of people in distress and the doctors caring for them. The Dutch chocolate brand, Tony's Chocolonely, is another example of this model. The brand is differentiating itself in the market in part by its mission to end child labor, forced labor, and other forms of exploitation in the cocoa industry. The company's mission is to make all chocolate worldwide 100 percent slavery-free. This goal is very present in the brand's actions in the market and its communication with customers, therefore, not only does it impact their supply chain strategies, but also helps create a demand side benefit leading to good growth. In 2018 the brand captured 18 percent of the market share in the Netherlands.

Notice that the models on the left in Figure 6.2, particularly "generating resources" or "changing mindsets," are less dependent on the product or service. As a result, we see more of these efforts among established, older, and leading brands because they are easier to adopt and implement. You do not need to change your business model, supply chain, ingredients, or packaging. All you need to do is promote and partner. Therefore, those actions, while they can be impactful, are also harder to differentiate. Using models to the right of the framework, particularly "enhancing alternatives," requires a deeper and longer-lasting commitment to the social impact effort. They can be more differentiating and offer a greater competitive advantage but harder to implement and sustain.

In practice, the different models of social impact by brands are not mutually exclusive. Managers often combine different areas in the design of their societal benefits. The combinations of impact areas can amount to the formation of three types of brands. First, there are brands we call "Agents of Change." They seek to change their own products and practices as their method for achieving a social impact. They do not engage as much in mainstream communication with consumers about their efforts. Instead, they orient engagement efforts towards key stakeholders and employees. While not exclusively, many of the brands within the Procter and Gamble portfolio have embedded social impact into their plans via an "agent of change" approach. Through programs like Ariel Cool Clean, promoting no prewashing for dishwashing in their Cascade commercials, encouraging the use of cold water for washing clothes in their Tide commercials, or using ocean-recovered plastic in their packaging for Head & Shoulders, they are focusing on shifting consumer behavior towards more environmentally friendly practices or products. Yet, their value proposition remains centered on product efficacy and performance, the core decision driver in many of the categories where they compete.

"Advocates of Change" are brands that focus more on external influence, primarily through storytelling and fundraising. A brand we consider to be exemplary in this category is Nike with its work on equality. Their campaign celebrating the former 49ers quarterback Colin Kaepernick's stand against police violence found a unique way of expanding the meaning of their "Just Do It" line beyond sports. They followed that effort with the promotion of a variety of statements by celebrity athletes in support of greater equality and inclusion.

In this case, Nike used its storytelling capability in partnership with their long-term agency, Weiden + Kennedy, to act as an advocate for social change. The female hygiene brand Always followed a similar path with their work on women empowerment. As discussed earlier, their advertising and social media campaign entitled "Like a Girl" advocated for a new perspective of girls in sports. Finally, the beer brand Tecate used their Superbowl ad investment and advertising activity in Mexico to advocate against domestic violence. The focus of these brands is on using their communication and consumer engagement skills to raise awareness or generate in support of a societal need. Yet, advocate brands stop short of utilizing all the available levers of change available to non-profit or government organizations. For instance, they aren't publicly involved in regulatory or policy changes.

In contrast, a final type of brand we call "Activists of Change" are brands that take comprehensive action towards the resolution, not only the awareness, of a societal issue. Brands following an "Activist of Change" model use similar storytelling techniques as advocate brands, but they go beyond advocacy and get directly involved in policy changes or market interventions to address a specific societal need. Consider the case of Patagonia and their frequent efforts to call attention to environmental protection causes. In 2014 they produced a documentary film about the negative environmental effects of hydropower. The "DamNation" documentary was part of an effort that

Figure 6.6 Example of Nike's advertising promoting equity in sports.

started 20 years earlier by Patagonia leaders to lobby for the removal of aging and damaging dam infrastructures. These sort of actions by a brand exceed the levels of involvement of advocacy and share instead the traits of social or environmental activism by organizations like Greenpeace or M.A. D.D. We see similar commitments to change by REI, a retail brand of outdoor equipment and sportswear. Also, the work over the last two decades by the Dove brand has certainly extended beyond changing mindsets. Through their work with educators, they have committed to changing behaviors, improving conditions, and generating resources in support of self-esteem for girls. Lastly, the bottled water brand Bonafont in Mexico has gone beyond advertising and general advocacy to behave like an activist for women's rights and empowerment. These brands incorporate most, if not all areas of impact into their creation of societal benefits.

Deciding on the combination of social benefits will enable managers to be clearer on the type of programs and partnerships they need as they move from strategy into the planning and implementation of their social impact. These classification schemes can help managers connect their chosen social-impact mission with specific market programs or interventions, as well as determine necessary partnerships they will need to effectively design and execute their programs.

Creating the Social Mission Statement

The social-mission statement is a simple way for managers to capture their social-impact strategy and communicate it to internal and external stakeholders. The statement has three elements: An articulation of the societal need the brand will "fight for or against." For instance, as we will discuss in a later chapter, leaders at SunTrust Bank decided to "fight against" financial stress and insecurity. Then comes a description of the main "enemy" or problem area within the broader societal need. For SunTrust, the "enemy" was a lack of knowledge among specific communities that historically have been underserved or underrecognized by the financial sector. Finally, managers need to clarify the social-impact model they will use to create a societal benefit. SunTrust focused on helping people learn about financial planning. The template provides the structure of a societal impact mission and can help managers define and communicate it to others:

"We will fight for (or against)/to _____ by _____ with _____."

To illustrate its use, consider how the social mission statement is applied in different scenarios and brands. The water and housing products multinational brand Lixil, for example, focuses on reducing poor sanitation related illnesses. Its social mission can be expressed as:

"We will fight for the eradication of illnesses resulting from poor sanitation systems in Sub-Saharan African communities by expanding access to safe and affordable toilets with the creation of an affordable new product line that meets the needs of communities without a clean sanitation infrastructure."

With clarity on its mission, managers would be ready to move to the last step of the social impact strategy process—the definition of the business logic.

Chapter 7

Clarify the Business Logic

"We want to help the polar bear—a beloved Coca-Cola icon since 1922—by conserving its Arctic habitat," said Muhtar Kent, Chairman and CEO of The Coca-Cola Company. *"That's why we're using one of our greatest assets—our flagship brand, Coca-Cola—to raise awareness for this important cause. And by partnering with WWF, we can truly make a positive difference for these majestic animals."*[1]

That statement was part of the announcement by The Coca-Cola Company in 2011 when they partnered with the World Wildlife Foundation (WWF) to raise funds for the construction of a refuge for polar bears. But why? Why would a soft drink company spend resources to support conservation efforts of this sort? Of course, this is not any soft drink, but one of the most well-known brands in the world. Also, they have been using the polar bear in their advertising since the 1920s. There was a clear brand fit with the cause. At the time, the melting of ice caps was endangering the habitat of polar bears, and the news was increasing awareness and concerns by the public. But is it fair to argue...why should Coke get involved? And particularly, why do it in such a consumer-facing way?

When answering questions about the reason for social impact programs, managers often allude to a moral case. For instance, because the brand has been using the polar bears' image in their advertising, they feel a responsibility to protect them. Such an explanation makes sense to external stakeholders and the press. But internally, leaders of social impact programs need to go beyond the moral case and clarify a business case. Otherwise, managers might struggle to convince other decision makers of the rationale for diverting resources and attention from the core responsibility of growing the business. The Coca-Cola Arctic Home program was both an effort to build a refuge for polar bears, and a program that could provide a commercial advantage to their business. However, the logic for the partnership is not immediately obvious from the outside. People might think that the business intent might have focused on building an emotional connection with consumers in a way that would provoke greater love and loyalty for the brand. While that might be true, such arguments rarely win sustained investment

DOI: 10.4324/9781003383246-8

and support because they are grounded on intangible assets or benefits that are difficult to measure.

Consider instead a different business logic by thinking about the commercial window the brand has during the winter holiday in North America. For many years, Coke has built a strong association with Christmas, partly through its continuous use of Santa in its advertising. Images of Santa in red with a Coke in hand are pervasive across supermarkets and Coca-Cola packages in North America and many other parts of the world. It is a marketing asset that the company uses across countries to drive consumption during the holidays—a time when traditional sales of soft drinks in the Northern hemisphere were lower, owing to colder temperatures. But what is the limitation of using Santa as an asset? The commercial activation window lasts approximately four weeks, between the end of November to the end of December. It makes little commercial sense to bring messages of Santa in early November or to leave them in the market after Christmas Day. That imposes a limitation on the use of the asset because the company has three to four weeks to generate a return on the investment from all the Santa programs. Now, consider the polar bear. It also carries associations with the winter holiday but is not constrained by holiday dates. With the polar bear activations, the commercial teams could generate programs with a longer store life. In fact, the promotion started in October and ended in February. That meant a significant reduction in cost by extending the market presence of the program. The cans, packaging, store merchandising, and other promotional material could enter and exit the market at a pace more in line with the manufacturing process.

A separate part of the business logic related to the trial and adoption of the brand among families. Consumer research showed the program tested well and increased purchase intent among parents, an important consumer group for the brand. It also presented an opportunity for the customer teams, particularly those responsible for large retailers such as Walmart or 7-Eleven. These account teams now had a unique program to offer retail customers in an effort to obtain additional visible space in the stores, a critical lever for growth.

So why did Coke invest resources, time, and money in partnering with the WWF to protect polar bears? Was it to generate a new commercial advantage? Was it to protect an animal they had promoted for almost a century? Was it both? The program generated significant awareness among the public of the challenges facing polar bears and their ecosystem. It was successful in raising funds needed to build the Arctic refuge. In addition, research we conducted among WWF donors showed they were largely supportive and enthusiastic about the partnership. At the same time, the program drove a 1 percent growth in sales while competitors experienced close to a 5 percent decline. It also resulted in close to 10 percent growth in revenue from the primary retail customers. When evaluated together, the Arctic Home program is an example of good growth. One of the reasons for its success was the broad adoption and integration it experienced across the Coca-Cola system, which is only possible in the presence of a clear business case.

When thinking about social impact programs managers often struggle to define commercial benefits. In many of our interviews, we frequently heard managers say that social impact programs should be done "because it is the right thing to do." At times they argue that a social impact investment transcends the business benefit and needs to be pursued regardless of its commercial implications. Yet, when working in a for-profit organization, grounding a social impact strategy on moral grounds can become a very limiting approach. If the creation of societal benefits is not accompanied by a robust business case like any other investment for the brand, it may receive initial support but is unlikely to have a lasting effect. This explains why so many social impact programs by brands are launched with much fanfare but reduced to Instagram posts in one calendar cycle. Effective social impact that lasts and results in material benefits for both the brand and society, requires a business case.

In the case of the Vaseline Healing Project that we reviewed earlier, Kathleen Dunlop was thrilled with the potential of creating a program that could increase the availability of Vaseline in situations of dire need, like refugee camps. However, she knew that to gain the resources and management support for the program's activation in the marketplace, she needed a business case. The social problem was clear, but what business problem could the Healing Project address? Brand awareness of Vaseline was high, and the product experienced deep in-market penetration. However, over time, managers worried that while the brand was present in millions of bathrooms, it was rarely used. As one manager put it, "Many people remember they have a Vaseline jar when they see it while packing to move to a new home." Importantly, they need to remind users of the role that Vaseline plays in taking care of dry skin before problems emerge or in helping heal cuts or minor injuries. Other moisturizing lotion brands were taking the skin protection association away from them. The healing project could help Kathleen achieve this business goal by reminding people of some of Vaseline's core functional benefits for the skin. Still, the question remained whether achieving this business goal would be more effective via the creation and promotion of the Healing Project or via more traditional programs to promote product features and benefits. The only way to find out was to conduct a market test. So, as she would have done with any other promotional investment, Kathleen hired a market research agency to conduct a test of various campaign options. They agreed upfront on the decision criteria for the Healing Project—it needed to outperform other options in driving awareness of Vaseline skin protection benefits and increasing purchase intent. The team anxiously awaited the results. They knew that unless the Healing Project was objectively a better investment for advancing the business goals, they might not be able to secure the funding and support to implement it in the marketplace. It comes down to opportunity costs, particularly when the funding comes from the operating units' brand budget and not a corporate reputation department. When the results came in, the Vaseline Healing Project performed significantly better than the other more product-focused campaigns. Kathleen and her team now had the data needed to create the internal business case, secure management support, and eventually build and implement the brand's first social impact program.

Social impact initiatives without a clear business case tend to struggle to sustain resource support and attention. Consider the example of Tecate, a leading beer brand in Mexico. Recognizing the link between alcohol consumption and the country's pervasive gender-violence problem, the Tecate team committed the brand to influencing change. The resulting campaign warned Tecate customers, "If you don't respect women, you are not one of us." Unveiled at a managers' meeting, the campaign received a standing ovation. Employees, activists, and the government celebrated the campaign, and it won numerous industry awards. It was also the last action Tecate took against gender violence. A year later, the brand returned to its traditional marketing efforts, including a vast boxing sponsorship. The campaign was motivated by well-intended and inspirational leaders who wanted to address a negative externality of their industry. The moral case was clear. The business case was not. Was this an effort to recruit new drinkers? What impact will it have on current drinkers? Would people who celebrated their actions be non-drinkers and, therefore, never planning to enter their franchise? There was no obvious way by which the actions, while helping raise awareness about an important issue, could also help the business. In that sense, Tecate behaved more like a non-profit organization in its efforts to fight for the reduction of domestic violence. Although it is a very commendable and important task, the design of the strategy was not complete because the business logic was not established. For instance, if the campaign for no-violence was accompanied with the introduction of a non-alcoholic version of Tecate, they could have attracted a segment of the market similar to that of its sister brand Heineken 0.0. To some readers, this push toward a business logic for social impact investments may feel excessive, uncomfortable, or even wrong. There can be a desire to stop at the moral case, as if it might make the action more authentic, more credible, more pure. But when seeking to create a societal benefit within the confines of a for-profit organization, we believe the leaders have a responsibility to design strategies that not only result in good deeds, but also good growth.

Unfortunately, many social impact efforts have a similar life cycle to what Tecate leaders experienced. They start with a realization of responsibility followed by a campaign, all of which is supported by a moral case—the need to invest because it is the right thing to do. This approach is effective at motivating one project, but it rarely leads to the development of a sustained program, let alone a material impact on the social need or the creation of a competitive advantage for the brand. Without a clear business rationale, even popular corporate initiatives will struggle for resources and languish over time.

Importantly, the business logic supporting a social impact strategy should be based on tangible and direct contributions to growth. It is tempting to argue that social impact will have a long-term benefit on the brand's reputation or increase the engagement or emotional connection between a brand and its consumers. However, while these arguments might be both viable and important, they are grounded on intangible benefits that are difficult to translate into financial statements or use to estimate a return on investment. Instead, our research into companies with sustained programs that generate good growth driving both market and social impact reveals successful managers build their business cases around a combination of three arguments— *strengthening the core, extending the brand or disrupting the market.*

A business case focusing on strengthening the core needs to find social impact elements that reinforce existing product attributes or generate new benefits to help differentiate the existing business. Consider the case of Chipotle. Until 2014, they were among the fastest-growing fast casual restaurants in the United States. In 2012—almost 20 years since its inception— Chipotle aired its first television commercial and advertising campaign. Was it to promote its great-tasting burritos? No. In fact, the product was not even included in the ad. Accompanied by Willie Nelson's voice singing "The Scientist," the animated video lasted about a minute and was shown during the broadcast of the American Music Awards. It told a story of the effects of modern agricultural processes on animal welfare and nature by highlighting the treatment of animals by large food corporations and presenting a vision of more sustainable practices followed by Chipotle and its network of farmers. The message went viral and became one of the most successful social media campaigns of the year. Their "food with integrity" mission, a staple of the company mission for years, became more present in the customer experience when visiting the restaurants. Signs announcing "food with integrity" could be seen on the menu boards and in stories written on their chip bags. But as we asked with the Coca-Cola Arctic Home program, why? Why would Chipotle invest millions in promoting a message that does not even show its product and, if anything, focuses on creating awareness about industrial agricultural processes and not its menu items?

We can find clues in the remarks by their founder and chairman at the time, Steve Ells, who was quoted in Fast Company in 2014, speaking about the role of their social impact mission. "Our investors are in it for only one reason," Ells stresses: "Great returns. They want to make money." As for store customers, the people buying millions of burritos across the country, "They care about taste, value and convenience. Somewhere down the line, they care about great customer service. They care about the design and the music of the restaurant. They care about lots and lots of little details." As for that food-with-integrity mission, "is it ever going to be the reason people come into the store? 'Oh, I want to eat food with integrity right now.' I don't think so." He seemed acutely aware that a social mission was not a direct driver of purchase. People would not go to Chipotle and have a burrito for lunch because of its social mission. They go because of great taste, first and foremost. And here is the key question—what drives the experience of great taste? Would the quality of ingredients impact your perception of taste? The data suggests as much, as do their messages. Notice the picture of the store sign taken at a Chipotle location back in 2014.

The framing of the message—is not about having more responsible, sustainable or healthy ingredients. It is all about taste. Their mission not only set them apart from any other alternative at the time, but also helped them compete on core attributes needed to win in their category—great taste and high-quality ingredients. Market research at the time showed they were significantly ahead of competitors on those critical dimensions. The Chipotle case is a clear example of social impact benefits used to strengthen a core attribute and competitive position of the brand.

Alternatively, managers can use social impact investments to extend the brand into adjacent categories, channels, or customer segments. For example, Heineken launched its Double Zero non-alcoholic beer as part of its commitment to support more responsible drinking. But it also used the launch to enter and gain market share from the adjacent market for non-alcoholic beverages that consumers were increasingly drinking. When interviewing marketing

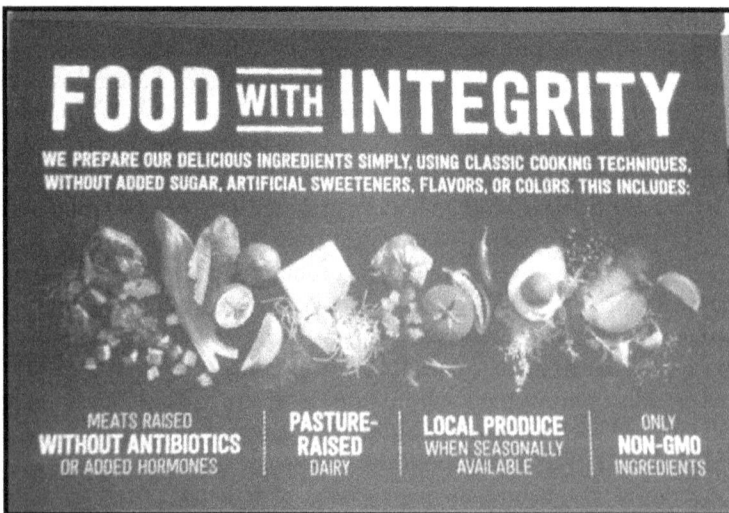

Figure 7.1 Image of a Chipotle store sign in 2014 describing the product ingredients.

leaders involved in the launch of Double Zero, they clarified their goal was not only to promote responsibility but also to grow the business in a new occasion and a new customer segment. They described the new occasion as the "second drink" moment. People at bars wanting a second drink but not wanting alcohol only had soft drinks or water as options. Heineken 0.0 gives them an option with the emotional benefit and taste of a beer while still enabling them to meet their alcohol consumption goal. That was a segment of the market they were not competing on and, therefore, became an opportunity for brand expansion. Likewise, fashion brand H&M has made sustainable design and production a key attribute of some product lines, including the Conscious line and the Re-Made collection. In doing so, the brand created new value for an eco-conscious customer segment, generated new revenues from sustainable product purchases, created new competitive differentiation, and reduced its environmental footprint.

One of the most successful cases of social impact for market expansion is the work we discussed earlier by Dove. It is frequently presented as an example of cause marketing or emotional storytelling, but the business case behind the campaign for Real Beauty is just as sound as the work they did to strengthen girls' self-esteem. Since its launch in 1957, Dove has positioned its brand not as a soap but as a beauty bar. Its main difference was the amount of moisturizing cream in the soap—specifically promoted as one-quarter moisturizing cream. That distinction left users with a softer feeling on their skin. While the specific communication methods changed from print to television, the product benefit remained the same for almost half a century. Then, in 2004, consumers in the United Kingdom were exposed to a new type of message from the brand. A series of billboards created by the advertising agency Ogilvy started to appear in the streets of London, Berlin, and other key cities in Europe. The message was not about ¼ moisturizing cream or dry skin. In fact, the message was not about soap at all. The product, central to their communication for almost 50 years, was completely absent. Instead, images of different types of women appeared with simple questions that challenged conventional views on beauty. As you can see in Figure 7.2, the messages carried only the brand name and a website directing people to the campaign for Real Beauty.

The program was the beginning of one of the most important repositioning efforts by a Unilever brand and, arguably, by any major consumer-packaged goods brand at the time. The work was led by Silvia Lagnado, then global marketing director for Dove. Seeking growth opportunities, she initiated a global study on women's beauty needs. The research, done in collaboration with social scientists at three universities, yielded a critical insight into an emerging need that had nothing to do with beauty products and everything to do with the beauty industry. Only 2 percent of women in the study reported feeling beautiful. Most women reported difficulty when trying to fit into the cultural standards of beauty.

□ grey?
□ gorgeous?

Why can't more women feel glad to be grey? Join the beauty debate.

campaignforrealbeauty.co.uk Dove

Figure 7.2 Examples of the initial phase in Dove's Real Beauty campaign.

□ wrinkled?
□ wonderful?

Will society ever accept 'old' can be beautiful? Join the beauty debate.

campaignforrealbeauty.co.uk Dove

□ fat?
□ fit?

Does true beauty only squeeze into size 8? Join the beauty debate.

campaignforrealbeauty.co.uk Dove

☐ flawed?
☐ flawless?

Is beautiful skin only ever spotless? Join the beauty debate.

campaignforrealbeauty.co.uk 🐦 | *Dove*

These struggles resulted in several negative effects on their well-being, including a lack of self-acceptance and self-esteem, particularly among the younger generation. The beauty and fashion industries, through their choice of models and messages, were promoting beauty in ways that destroyed it. Interestingly, this finding was not about understanding people as consumers of beauty products, but understanding the needs of consumers as people. By looking into the market through this new lens, Silvia and her team uncovered what they saw as a new mission for the Dove brand—to fight for Real Beauty. The idea resonated internally, but was the investment justified? How can they convince the business unit operators that they needed to divert resources originally reserved for growing their business and promoting their products into advocacy for real beauty? After all, Dove and Unilever were not a "non-profit" organization. They had a responsibility to both their shareholders and the communities they served.

The business logic is harder to see from the outside. At the time, Unilever initiated an effort to simplify its operations and reduce costs. Their acquisition of products around the world resulted in a portfolio that exceeded 1,500 brands. Each brand required different management solutions, shelf space, and attention. Significant efficiencies in marketing and selling costs could be achieved by creating what practitioners call "master brands." These are brands that stand for more general benefits instead of specific product solutions, enabling the firm to sell more products under fewer marketing and promotional efforts. Think of Nike, Apple, or Disney—brands with expansive portfolios of products across a diverse range of categories. In contrast, think of Coke, Pepsi, or, at the time, Dove. While these are successful brands, they operate within the constraints of one specific category of products. In the case of Dove, it was soap. But what if Unilever could reposition Dove not just as a brand competing in the soap segment but as a brand of products in an array of skincare and beauty segments? Shampoo, conditioners, face cleaners, skin lotions, body wash, and yes, soap. Developing Dove into a master brand required repositioning its meaning in the marketplace, away from a functional product like soap and towards a broader benefit of beauty that could transcend product categories. That is where the moral case and the business case connected. Yes, Ms. Langano's research found a societal need that Dove was uniquely positioned to fight for, given the company's heritage. At the same time, her profound understanding of the business needs helped her see the benefit of leveraging the program to extend the brand's position away from its traditional functional benefit. The result was good growth—the creation of one of the most successful brand transformations of the last 25 years. Internally, Ms. Lagnado used the business case to build financial support for the repositioning effort that enabled the brand to enter close to a dozen new product categories beyond soap. Externally, her team used the moral case to build support and partnerships with community organizations working on issues of self-esteem. Together, they implemented a program that, while evolving over time, continues to be central to the Dove brand. Data from Statista in Figure 7.3 shows the lasting impact of the repositioning—significantly expanding the role of personal care products in Unilever's business.

Notice the growth of the personal care products in Unilever's portfolio since the launch of the Real Beauty program which now accounts for close to 40 percent of the firm's revenues.

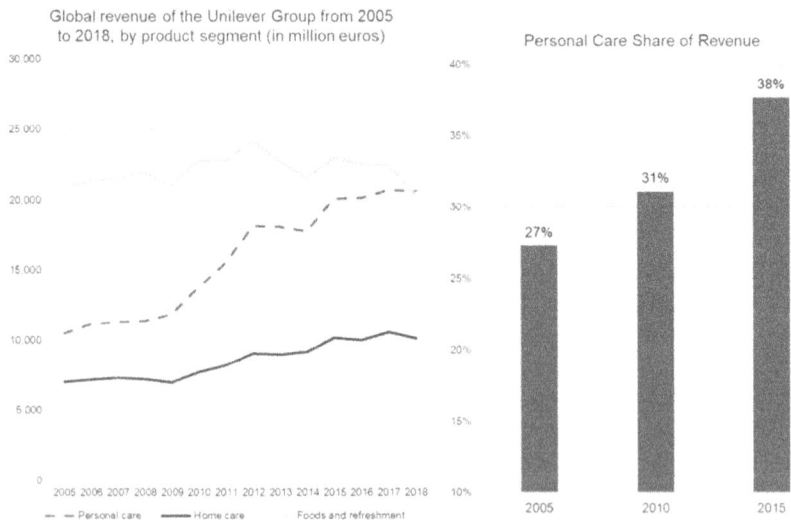

Figure 7.3 Results reported by the Unilever company for its personal care products during the type of the Real Beauty campaign.

Another brand that has leveraged social impact to extend its business is Seventh Generation. Initially, they were a laundry detergent brand, but since the acquisition by Unilever, they have expanded to become a platform brand with products across seemingly unrelated consumer goods categories. They now offer paper towels, baby products, surface and dish cleaners, deodorant, handwash, and feminine hygiene products. Can you imagine buying a line of paper towels under the Tide name? Or a deodorant branded Bounty? The footprint of Seventh Generation is impressive and potentially unachievable by traditional brands in each of those categories. What enables the brand managers to extend their core offerings so far beyond their original categories? The answer lies in their value proposition. Different from Tide or Bounty, their positioning is not tied to a product category definition or solution. Instead, their position centered on an environmental benefit delivered in the form of lower toxicity, natural ingredients, and recycled packaging materials. Those benefits are not relevant to everyone, but there is a sizable market that cares about the environmental impact of their homes or personal products. For them, Seventh Generation is not just a laundry detergent, but a brand of safe and responsible products across multiple uses and needs.

Another example of social impact that helps extend the brand is the case of CVS. In 2014 the retail drugstore chain removed tobacco-based products, including cigarettes, from its over 7,000 stores in the United States. Subsequent

Figure 7.4 Product portfolio of Seventh Generation.

research found that the change in availability of tobacco products was linked to material decreases in smoking. Specifically, the study by Polinski et al. (2017) found that households that purchased cigarettes exclusively at CVS Pharmacy were 38 percent more likely to stop buying cigarettes after CVS stopped tobacco sales. CVS Pharmacy frequent cigarette consumers deemed as "3-or-more-pack purchasers" were more than twice as likely to stop buying cigarettes, reflecting the greater disruption in their tobacco use and purchasing behaviors when CVS removed the product from their stores. Similarly, in the 13 states where CVS captured greater than or equal to 15 percent retail market share, consumers purchased 95 million fewer packs of cigarettes over the eight months subsequent to tobacco removal (equivalent to five fewer packs per smoker), representing a 1 percent reduction in sales in these states.[2]

That is strong evidence of social impact influenced by their decision. But the question is, why did CVS decide to give up on an estimated $2 billion dollars in revenue generated by the sales of tobacco products? And why did the value of the CVS stock increase upon the announcement? This counterintuitive result has to do with a new vision by the CEO at that time, Larry Merlo, for the expansion of the business. The leadership team saw a structural change in healthcare as a result of the passage of the Affordable Care Act in 2010. The market for healthcare services dramatically expanded with the inclusion of millions of people who had previously been uninsured. The country's infrastructure was not ready to support the heightened demand for services, and CVS saw an opportunity for expansion by providing entry-level healthcare services like the Minute Clinic. There, patients could get immunization shots or be seen by a qualified nurse practitioner for simple conditions and treatments. The move represented a new revenue stream for CVS that was, for the most part, complementary to their existing business. Yet, one product stood in the way of their credible play into healthcare—tobacco. Their exit from the tobacco business and the social impact it generated, in part, enabled their expansion into healthcare. This was a strong business case for a positive action in society.

The third way to design a business case for social impact is to see it as an enabler of market disruption. We often associate disruption with technology breakthroughs that enable a company to create an offering that others cannot easily replicate, at least in the short term. Think for instance, the effect of the iPad or iPhone entries on the market of personal digital devices. They were not only different, but better at performing critical tasks that resulted in years of roughly uncontested growth. A similar effect was caused by Uber in transportation or Airbnb in hospitality. In all these cases, the market disruption occurred by the introduction of new technologies that enabled new benefits, not immediately accessible to incumbents. The result is growth that not only leverages the market, but changes it.

Innovative pioneers and entrepreneurs have demonstrated that social impact, like technology, has the potential to disrupt markets and provide firms with a period of uncontested growth. Consider the case of Blueland which we introduced earlier in the book. Co-founded by Sarah Paiji Yoo and Syed Naqvi in 2019, the company brought to market a new way of providing household cleaning solutions including bathroom cleaners, kitchen cleaners, window cleaners, dish soap and detergents, among others. All under one brand name. All without plastic. Their mission was to take plastic out of the process of buying and using cleaning products at home. Normally, we buy a cleaning product in a plastic bottle and once it is used, we "throw it away." The problem is, there is no "away." "Away" often means our landfills. With their motto of "refills, no landfills"— Blueland was the first company to create the category of refillable cleaning products and bring the tablet format to market. Their model changed the game of selling and using cleaning products by enabling customers to get a starting kit which comes with durable, multi-use, 100 percent without bisphenol A (BPA-free) bottles. The product is delivered via tablets that come in compostable and biodegradable pouches. The boxes, tapes, packaging material, and product formulations have been designed to reduce environmental impact and eliminate plastic. When customers run out of the product, a new order arrives. All they do is take a tablet, place it in the bottle and add water. In a few minutes the product is ready to be used, and no empty plastic bottle is left behind in our landfills. In three years, the company sold more than 10 million products to over 1 million customers, generating more than $100 million in sales. In 2023 the company reported it reached profitability according to the website Retail Dive. It is now expanding its presence by distribution deals with Target and Costco. Now, imagine if you are Procter and Gamble trying to compete with Blueland and slow down their growth? Yes, you can drop prices to make the switch harder for consumers. But reinvent your business model…that will take years. All that time will be time that Blueland gets to grow, roughly uncontested, changing the rules of the game. That is market disruption, enabled by social impact. Fortunately, Blueland is not the only startup seeking to disrupt and find good growth in this way. Smyle, founded in 2020 by Almar Fernhout, Dennis Kamst, and Roger Nefkens started with a similar idea—in this case take plastic out of our oral care. They created a new way to deliver tooth cleaning products, without the paste. Using tablets in glass bottles, they are finding good growth by designing plastic out of the process. Fairfone is challenging the convention that a good phone means a new phone. The continuous pursuit of upgrades are leaving behind a significant tail of electronic waste. Their product is built to last, creating an offering that is slowly disrupting the rules of the game.

What BlueLand is doing to household cleaners, Planet A Foods is doing to the food industry, particularly in the business of ingredients. With a mission to create food alternatives with dramatically lower CO_2 emissions and environmental footprints, they seek to disrupt an industry dominated by giant corporations with vast resources but older operating models. They are currently focused on cocoa through a product they call Choviva. Back in 2021 one of their leading scientists, Sara Marquart, became aware of the significant sourcing concentration of cocoa beans in two African countries—Ghana and Côte d'Ivoire—where more than half of the world's supply of cocoa comes from. Both countries are experiencing weather changes as a result of climate change, including increases in rain that have damaged the harvest and impacted global availability and prices. Ms. Marquart, working with Anna-Lena Krug, another food scientist at Planet A Foods, saw the shortage as an opportunity to create an alternative to chocolate that, without sacrificing the taste, could offer a social impact advantage. After close to 800 recipe trials, they found in a combination of oats and sunflower seeds a new ingredient that looks like chocolate, tastes like chocolate, smells like chocolate, but has no cocoa. Their aim is not to replace chocolate in its most delicious and indulgent forms but rather to offer the industry an alternative for food products where chocolate is a peripheral ingredient, like in the case of cereals, ice cream, or candy. In doing so, alleviating the supply pressure on cocoa beans. They sell Choviva at similar prices to chocolate but significantly lower carbon emissions. Owing to its simple ingredients, it can be produced in many countries, including the northern hemisphere, eliminating the need for long-distance shipping. The agriculture process also consumes less water than cocoa trees, giving Choviva a unique and differentiating benefit in the market. Combining social impact with high quality and delicious taste is turning Planet A Food into a disruptive force in the ingredients business. Their next step is Palm Oil, an ingredient that has been a leading cause of significant environmental damage, including deforestation and reforestation, while becoming a pervasive ingredient of many consumer products.

Clarifying how a social-impact initiative will strengthen, extend or disrupt a market provides a path toward clarifying its business logic. In fact, selling into an organization a social impact program, particularly for the first time, is not often a barrier. But sustaining it or scaling it becomes unviable when the business logic is not prioritized, present, or grounded in tangible benefits. Comfort with the moral and business implications of social impact is, in fact, an important leadership trait of managers seeking to create good growth.

Social Impact Strategy Framework

Figure 7.5 presents the Social Impact Strategy Framework, which can help managers simplify the different choices involved in designing a social impact strategy. The Societal Needs are based on the UN Sustainable Development goals, a good starting point for crafting the Social Impact strategy. It then describe the choices of Brand Mission and Business Logic to complete the strategy process. Figure 7.6 presents an illustrative example of the framework application to the Brita case discussed in Chapter 4.

Societal Need		Brand Mission		Business Logic	
No Poverty: End poverty in all its forms everywhere.	◯				
Zero Hunger: End hunger, achieve food security and improved nutrition, and promote sustainable agriculture.	◯	Generate Resources	◯		
Good Health and Well-being: Ensure healthy lives and promote well-being for all at all ages.	◯			Strengthen the core	◯
Quality Education: Ensure inclusive and equitable quality education and promote lifelong learning opportunities for all.	◯				
Gender equality: Acheive gender equality and empower all women and girls.	◯	Change Mindsets	◯		
Clean Water and Sanitation: Ensure availability and sustainable management of water and sanitation for all.	◯				
Affordable and Clean Energy: Ensure access to affordable, reliable, sustainable, and modern energy for all.	◯				
Decent Work and Economic Growth: Promote sustained, inclusive, and sustainable economic growth, full and productive employment, and decent work for all.	◯				
Industry, Innovation, and Infrastructure: Build resilient infrastructure, promote inclusive and sustainable industrialization, and foster innovation.	◯	Influence Behavior	◯	Expand the business	◯
Reduced Inequalities: Reduce inequality within and among countries.	◯				
Sustainable Cities and Communities: Make cities and human settlements inclusive, safe, resilient, and sustainable.	◯				
Responsible Consumption and Production: Ensure sustainable consumption and production patterns.	◯	Enhance Options	◯		
Climate Action: Take urgent action to combat climate change and its impacts.	◯				
Life Below Water: Conserve and sustainably use the oceans, seas, and marine resources for sustainable development.	◯				
Life on Land: Protect, restore, and promote sustainable use of terrestrial ecosystems, manage forests, combat desertification, halt and reverse land degradation, and halt biodiversity loss.	◯			Disrupt the market	◯
Peace, Justice, and Strong Institutions: Promote peaceful and inclusive societies, provide access to justice for all, and build effective, accountable institutions at all levels.	◯	Improve Conditions	◯		
Partnerships for the Goals: Strengthen the means of implementation and revitalize the global partnership for sustainable development.	◯				

Figure 7.5 Social Impact Strategy Framework.

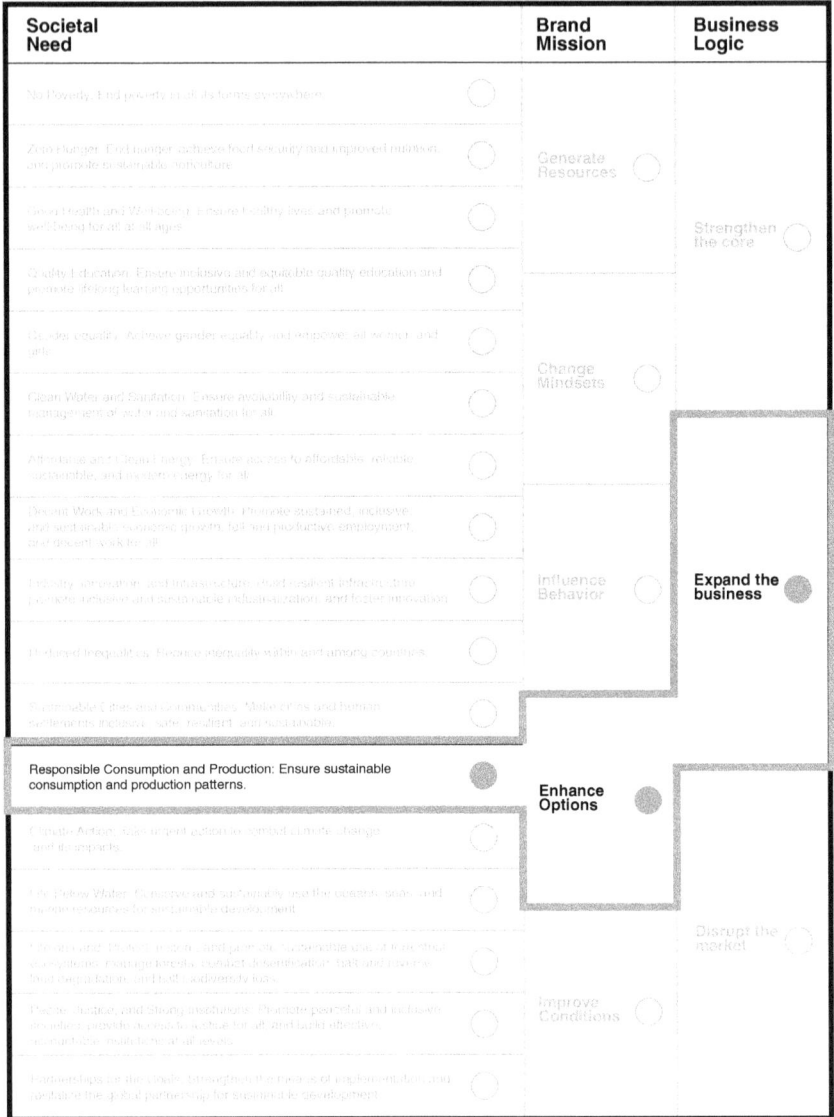

Figure 7.6 Social Impact Strategy Framework: Brita Example.

Notes

1 The Coca-Cola Company (2011, October 25). Iconic Coca-Cola red cans turn Arctic white. Coca-Cola Company.
2 Polinski, J. M., Howell, B., Gagnon, M. A., Kymes, S. M., Brennan, T. A., & Shrank, W. H. (2017). Impact of CVS Pharmacy's discontinuance of tobacco sales on cigarette purchasing (2012–2014). *American Journal of Public Health, 107*(4): 556–562.

Chapter 8

Communication Practices

What is the difference between a public service announcement and a social impact message? Unfortunately, often very little. Managers spend considerable time crafting brand messages that are engaging to their audiences and effective in driving specific goals. Increasingly, brand content is managed via a thorough process of experimentation, testing, and optimization. However, when it comes to social impact, it seems few of those methods are used, and instead, brand managers and their agencies focus more on the cause than their brands by adopting a public service framing in the way they communicate. This means sharing stories about their contribution to societal issues in ways that might create "goodwill" towards the company but maybe not "buywill" towards the brand.

We studied the engagement generated by hundreds of social impact media posts across 30 top brands in the United States and found that social impact messages had no effect on attitudinal engagement metrics such as "likes." Other research, such as the work by Lee, Hosanagar, and Nair (2014)[1] or Malhotra, Malhotra, and See (2013)[2], found social impact messages were having no effect or, at times, a negative effect on engagement. Such a muted response can be unexpected for managers who believe messages about "doing good" should receive more support than messages about "selling goods." But in fact, quite the opposite can happen. Messages intended to do good have generated negative responses from consumers or critics. The brand team at Gillette learned this firsthand when they launched a campaign to raise awareness about toxic masculinity. On January 13, 2019 Gillette released a short film entitled "The best a man can be." It was a new take on their historical tagline, "The best a man can get," but this time, the focus was not on the quality of the shave. Instead, the message showcased negative men's behaviors such as sexual harassment, mansplaining, catcalling of women, or bullying. Its opening said "...*Bullying, the #MeToo movement against sexual harassment, toxic masculinity...is this the best a man can be? We can't hide from it. It's been going on far too long. We can't laugh it off, making the same old excuses...boys will be boys.*"

DOI: 10.4324/9781003383246-9

It then proceeded to present situations where men behaved differently and, according to Gillette, better. It ended with a call for men to educate the next generation in ways that will help eliminate the behaviors of the past. The message struck a chord among some, but it also ignited a controversy. By August of the same year, the video had been viewed over 30 million times, and while it generated 800,000 likes, it had about double the number of dislikes. The comments section was filled with people claiming to stop buying Gillette products and criticizing the brand for preaching morals in their ads. Four years later, negative comments could still be found on social media. For instance:

"Wow, this commercial made me realize that I'm a misogynist! I'm going to buy more Gillette! Said no sane person ever, lol."

"This commercial doesn't say all men are bad. It says only 99.9 percent of men are toxic."

"I remember when I stopped buying Gillette products."

"Since when has shaving something to do with sexual harassment."

When their annual report was published, the business effect became more apparent. The Medium reported that Gillette experienced the biggest drop in market share since the brand was acquired by P&G in 2005, and their sales of grooming products experienced a 6.5 percent decline vs. 2018. We can't attribute these results solely to the campaign and its controversy. Gillette products were under significant threat by lower priced entries like Dollar Shave Club and Harris during the same time period. However, the results changed the performance trajectory of the prior decade, and managers at Gillette decided it was time to change. By August of the same year, leaders began to announce a change in direction. *We are shifting the spotlight from social issues to local heroes,*" read the news headline on August 22, 2019. While it is not possible to get accurate measures of the specific impact of the campaign on the brand, its lack of continuity sends a strong signal that the effort did not have the desired effect.

Gillette is not the only brand that has experienced the negative consequence of a social impact campaign. More recently, BudLight and Target have seen similar backlash in response to their efforts to be more inclusive of the LGBTQ+ community in their messages or products. Yet, avoiding social impact messages because others have been criticized is like avoiding launching new products because others have failed. We know there are brands like Dove or Nike that have disrupted markets and moved consumers with their social impact messages. So, the real question is, what is the difference between social impact messages that move us to like and buy a brand vs. those we ignore or criticize? In this chapter, we will cover five principles behind social impact messages that work and help avoid some of the most common pitfalls and challenges present when seeking good growth.

Ensure Authenticity

Was it authentic for Pepsi to create an ad about social justice? It is a difficult question to answer, in part because authenticity can be hard to define. However, questions about the authenticity of a social impact effort can threaten the success of programs and significantly increase the risk of backlash. It is uncommon for managers to be overly concerned about authenticity when creating content for their brands. Many of them have built successful careers by finding new customer needs, identifying and introducing new product features and services, or crafting messages to drive trial or purchase. Authenticity can feel like a soft, intangible, and impractical concern. Equally important, managing and behaving in the market in a way that is understood as authentic can be challenging when other commercial goals and competitive pressures are at play. Recent research on the subject provides guidance on how to incorporate this critical consideration in the creation of social impact content. In a review of 25 years of academic research on brand authenticity, Jonatan Södergren defined brand authenticity as 'the extent to which consumers perceive a brand to be faithful and true toward itself and its consumers (Morhart et al., 2015). He reports two general antecedents of authenticity for a brand. The first is consistency with prior behavior. In other words, is the social impact program consistent with the brand's past? If Nike had communicated about social issues in the past, it is more likely that its efforts to communicate about equality would be perceived as authentic. At the same time, if Adidas had never made social impact part of their communication, the first time they did it, they might experience a heightened risk of being perceived as inauthentic. It is particularly important for managers to be knowledgeable about their brand heritage as they are making choices on social impact. At Coke, the brand leaders often spent time in the archives of the company, studying the history of their actions over decades to better define the spaces of societal benefits that would be most suited for their brands. In other words, a connection with the past guides their design for social impact programs. When they decided to launch the Arctic Home program, they chose to do it in natural history museums in part because the venue was a more authentic way of discussing the issue. Details like these nurture authenticity.

As discussed earlier in the book, a second critical driver of authenticity is the perception of fit between the societal message and the products or services the brand sells. Research finds that consumers have an easier time making sense of a societal impact effort when there is a logic to the brand action. That logic is more easily formulated if the societal benefit is related to the product benefit. For instance, for over 50 years, Dove has positioned its brand of soap on the concept of beauty. In fact, they called their product a beauty bar instead of a soap bar. Therefore, a societal benefit related to the perception of beauty was easy to align with the product they sold.

Importantly, Dove did not have a history of societal benefits prior to the launch of the Real Beauty campaign. There was nothing in their heritage to support the authenticity of their program. However, the societal need they sought to address was naturally connected to their offering, therefore ensuring product-cause fit. In essence, effective social impact messages are authentic social impact messages. Nurturing authenticity in your communication ensures that you select areas that are consistent with the heritage of your past or the benefits of your present.

Design Interventions

Alex Thompson and Pio Schunker did not know each other. However, they had a similar role as leaders of public relations and communications, one at the retailer REI and the other for Coca-Cola. They were both charged with communicating the social impact efforts of their brands in the market. Importantly, they both rejected the idea of creating a campaign and challenged their teams with a different question. Instead of asking "what can we say to consumers?" about our social impact efforts, they asked their teams, "What can we do?". By changing the question, they unlocked the potential of their teams and brands to create a higher level of social impact, one based on interventions, not just communications. In the case of REI, Alex sought a way to demonstrate the retail chain's commitment to the environment. By asking, "What can we do?" he avoided the typical campaign with statements of beliefs or reports of contributions. Instead, they found a dramatically novel way to make clear what matters most to REI. We will explain more about that in a moment.

A few years earlier, Pio Schunker was facing a similar need as head of creative for Coca-Cola USA. He was charged with finding a way of communicating the brand's partnership with the World Wildlife Foundation. Initially, he followed a more common path of action by briefing agency partners to create campaign ideas. After reviewing a first round of options, he found nothing to be good enough, big enough, or clear enough. They all suffered from the public service announcement problem. Nothing was intrinsically wrong with them, but nothing was interesting either. Given the state of the creative process, most leaders would have changed agencies and looked for different people and ideas. Instead, he challenged the brief itself and made the same change that Alex unknowingly did a few years later. He changed the question and asked his agency team to think about what Coke "could do" to demonstrate, not just communicate, its partnership with the WWF. The revised presentation was filled with promotional and event ideas. One of the slides had an image in the upper right-hand corner that captured Pio's imagination. It was the image of a Coca-Cola can in white. Pio saw that and jumped—"That's it. That is our action. For the first time in our history, we will change the color of our cans to support the Polar Bears."

The discussion materialized in the goal of raising $10 million dollars to help the WWF create a refuge for Polar Bears in the Arctic. That moment was the start of what became the Arctic Home program, which we discussed in greater depth in an earlier chapter.

Alex's experience at REI followed a similar path. REI, a nationwide retailer dedicated to outdoor gear and lifestyle, has a history of supporting environmental conservation. For instance, they have led advocacy efforts calling for legislation that will protect and steward public lands, increase accessibility to parks, and reduce factors impacting climate change. Alex was charged with finding a new way of communicating REI's social impact to their employees and customers. Avoiding the common path of a traditional communication brief to an agency, he instead asked his team what action REI could take to unambiguously demonstrate, not just communicate, their social impact. The answer was as unconventional as the question. Close the store for a day and encourage customers and employees to go outside instead. But not any day. The key was to close the store the day no one else would—Black Friday. It was a day that represented, for many retailers, the highest sales for the year. Black Friday—the day after the Thanksgiving holiday in the United States—is a day when, traditionally, many consumers go to stores to shop for Holiday gifts. News reports of people lining up to enter stores at midnight or 3 am were common. Also common were stories of people fighting in stores for products that were running out of stock. All of these images represented consumerism at its extreme, creating the perfect contrast for what REI wanted to communicate—the value of enjoying the outdoors. And so, the "Get Outside" program began. The first time they did it, Alex's team created a simple message on social media with their CEO announcing their decision to close on Black Friday and an invitation for people to follow suit. The story of their action captivated the internet and became the most viral message they had created. It became news. It became a reference. Soon after, other retailers followed, and a countermovement to the commercial side of Black Friday was born.

As we discussed in Chapter 2, a common managerial mistake is to think of a social-impact strategy as promoting a brand's social responsibility or sustainability efforts instead of addressing a social need. In our studies of effective social-impact efforts, we found that they focused on interventions with tangible, often bold, social, or environmental actions.

Plan for Precision over Scale

Once you have clarity on the message you want to communicate, then it is time to introduce it in the market. The question is how? Traditional playbooks for increasing demand focus on reach by exposing the greatest number of potential customers to a product message. But social impact communications work differently—they are not about scale, but precision.

Given the variety of social needs, the potential for politicization, and the challenge of balancing social-need-oriented messages with more commercial ones, the traditional playbook can lead you to communicate at the wrong time or to the wrong audience—both of which can increase the chances of a backlash. Instead, plan for precision by identifying the right audience, timing, and framing of your message.

When deciding on the best audience for your social impact message, it is critical to consider the knowledge and experience that different customer segments have with your brand. Our research shows a concave relationship between brand usage and the effect of social impact. It is highest among people who occasionally consume your product or service. For instance, in a study on the effects of sustainable agriculture, recycled packaging, and nutritional benefits of juice drinks on consumers, we found the effect on brand equity was 2.5 times greater among people who consumed the brand once a month or less than for those that consumed it weekly. The results suggest that regular users of a brand are already familiar with its offering, and the social impact information does little to alter their decision to use a product. Importantly, we find low to no effect among people who do not use a brand or product. In other words, on average, it appears that social impact messages are most effective at increasing consideration, not creating it. In fact, if you reach non-users with a social impact message, it might increase the odds of criticism because they may be unfamiliar with your brand heritage and, therefore, doubt your intentions. These results might vary by product category and, therefore, are important to study during the social impact strategy stage. However, our research to date suggests that it might be better to focus your audience planning on light users and, to the greatest extent possible, avoid reaching non-users with your social impact messages.

The next step of precision in your communication planning involves the moment and timing of your message. There are two timing considerations to take into account. The first concerns the moment in the customer journey. For example, Timberland's brand team was working on the launch of a new line of boots with recycled rubber soles. The question was when and how to share the message, so it was most relevant for customers. Should they target a broad audience across media, place the messaging at the storefront, or share it only when customers try the boots in-store? Their research yielded a surprise: telling people about the recycled soles didn't get them to go to the store or try on the boots. But, if they were already in the store and *did* try them on, learning at that moment about the sustainable soles increased the chance of purchase. Another moment in the customer journey that has received a lot of attention is the checkout or payment. Many retailers or service providers have adopted the practice of soliciting donations to charity as part of the payment process. Research by Adam Hepworth, Na Young Lee, and Alex Zablah found that soliciting donations at checkout increased customers' anxiety and reduced their evaluations of the service. They state:

> "Our results reveal that such anxiety decreases during solicitation episodes when customers agree to donate; however, this occurs only when frontline employees make the requests rather than self-checkout technologies. These results caution managers that checkout charity solicitations may have unintended consequences on customers that result in negative encounter outcomes, particularly in service environments in which the solicitation is technology-mediated."

The precise moment for communicating a social impact benefit will vary by product and industry, but it helps to decide the role of the societal benefit in a brand's growth strategy. Will social impact play a central or peripheral role in the position of the brand in the market? If serving markets that are highly motivated by social concerns, then social impact may play a central role in the value proposition. For instance, the startup Nothing New is looking to disrupt the traditional footwear market with high social-impact offerings—shoes made from recycled cotton, fishing nets, rubber, plastic, and cork. Even the packaging is made from 100 percent recycled paper. Given the centrality of social impact on their positioning, the messages are embedded across different communication channels that customers experience, including social media, website, and in-store.

Other brands choose or migrate to peripheral positioning. Warby Parker, for instance, has made expanding eye care in developing countries a core part of its business. In the early days of their venture, their societal benefit was a central claim made to investors, employees, and customers, and it became a key reason people wanted to work for the company. Therefore, it was front and center in their website and product communication. However, over time, they discovered that expanding eye care was not the main reason people wanted to buy from them. In order to compete, the brand needed to win at design, price, and convenience, not at social impact. Did they drop their commitment to expanding eye care? Not at all. They simply shifted the role it played in the demand side from central to peripheral—visible to interested customers but not central in the brand's messaging. Therefore, if social impact is a core way in which you will differentiate in the market, like in the case of Tom's or Allbirds, then embed it into the customer experience journey, particularly in those moments designed to generate consideration.

Make It Clear You Care

Consumers know that when a company introduces a new product, they do it to make money. The commercial interests involved in the day-to-day marketing of products and services are acknowledged and expected. But that expectation can come into direct conflict with the notion of societal benefits. An important challenge for managers when competing on social impact is that the consumer will question their intentions, not just their actions. Consumers may recognize the value in the brand's societal efforts but still question their motivation as being commercially driven. That seed of doubt and suspicion of what economists call manipulative intent can significantly inhibit the success of a social impact program.

In a recent meta-analysis of consumer responses to cause marketing campaigns,[3] the authors reported numerous studies that found signals of sincerity to be a key component in the design of social impact communications. They define signals of sincerity as providing evidence in your communication that the brand's motives are altruistic rather than profit-oriented, which is not the norm when it comes to managing marketing resources. However, unless consumers perceive your social impact efforts to be sincere, coming from a true and genuine interest in the societal issue, the likelihood of success decreases. Keep in mind that sincerity and authenticity are distinct factors to manage. Authenticity, as discussed earlier, is about the social impact benefit of being true to your heritage or your business. Sincerity is about demonstrating an intrinsic interest in the societal issue beyond profit. A study of movie ticket sales in China published in 2017[4] provides some clues as to why. Dube, Luo, and Fang find that the combination of promotional discounts with charitable donations can decrease the demand for products. They explain the results based on the warm-glow theory, suggesting that consumers are willing to buy products with charitable components, owing in part to the positive feeling they derive from supporting a cause. The warm-glow theory was introduced by economist James Andreoni in 1989 to explain altruistic behavior by arguing that people derive a personal sense of satisfaction or "warm glow" from the act of giving or helping others. The study by Dube suggests that if the charity act is perceived as commercial and not philanthropic, the warm-glow effect is dampened. Therefore, when managing the design of a social impact program, it is imperative to be, and be perceived as, sincere in your intention to support the cause. The question is how. The first step of the answer is not surprising—you need to personally care. A brand's social impact is really the social impact created by the people that manage it. Therefore, you as a leader of a brand need to genuinely care for the societal need you seek to support with your brand. It may seem obvious, but it is not uncommon for managers to venture into social impact work by treating it as any other investment, without personally connecting with the issue at hand. In fact, we would go as far as say that if you do not personally and collectively genuinely care for a societal need, move on. Don't make it part of your brand. Now, operating out of genuine care does not mean others will see it that way. Research into the topic provides some guidance about how to ensure consumers correctly perceive your commitment. One common alternative is increasing the size of the social impact benefit, as the greater the donation or action, the greater the sincerity. However, research finds conflicting evidence in the relationship between perceived intention and the size of the contribution. A study by Arora and Henderson (2007)[5] found a positive impact of donations on consumers' purchase intent, but that impact was not altered by the size of the donation. Dube et al. (2017) finds that the effect on purchase increases with the donation size. Given the lack of consistent findings, it is not clear that the amount of your impact matters as much as the presence of it. However, a strong contributor to sincerity is a fit between the brand and the social impact area. We discussed the importance of fit in earlier chapters, and this reiterates why it should become a core criterion in the design of a social impact message. If the social impact area is related to your product or brand associations and it is easy for consumers to make sense of, it is less likely that consumers will question its intention in the market.

Another source of sincerity is a product's role in the social impact message. Marketing managers are used to creating messages with their product at the center of the content or story. However, research has found that when it comes to social impact messaging, it is best to put the product on the sidelines. The more central the product role is in a social impact story, the greater the chances of the perceived commercial intent eroding perceptions of sincerity. Successful social impact campaigns such as the ones by Dove Real Beauty, Chipotle Food with Integrity, and Always Like a Girl have all made the social impact area the star of their stories, with the brand as endorser. This clearly creates a challenge because the expectation by managers is that communication funds are used to sell the product and to do so, they need to show the product. One solution is to find balance in the portfolio of messages and accompany social impact actions with other messages that are geared towards generating demand. For instance, when Dove launched the Real Beauty campaign, they also had other messages, including in-store and online, where they promoted relevant product features.

A final signal of sincerity is how concrete your social impact benefit is. This is particularly relevant when brands choose to express support in social media. A study[6] by Chintagunta, Kansal, and Pachigolla of brand responses to the Black Lives Matter movement after the murder of George Floyd found that immediacy of support was not as important as specificity of support in provoking positive response by consumers. They state:

> "Most companies started by issuing a 'words only' statement of support for the cause, which was usually not well received by customers, and many of them led to an increase in negative sentiment. Only when the companies pledged actual investments did the negative sentiment reduce."

Frame To Engage

For this last factor we need to review research into something that is less common for communication and brand managers to consider—message construal, or how people make sense of information. Academics studying the effectiveness of messages have used construal-level theory (CLT) to explain consumer responses and reactions. It refers to the temporal, spatial, or social distance of consumers' mental formations and argues that people construe the same information asymmetrically depending on its psychological distance (Trope and Liberman, 2010[7]). CLT proposes that the more distant an object or event is, the more likely it is to be represented in terms of abstract features, which are referred to as high-level construal (Trope and Liberman, 2010). Alternatively, low-level construal occurs as temporal distance decreases and the object is considered via more detailed and concrete features (Trope and Liberman, 2010). An easy way of thinking about this distinction is thinking about the forest vs. the trees. CLT stipulates that consumers will draw on more abstract features when describing future events, or think more about the forest. In contrast, they will rely on more concrete features to represent an event in closer temporal distance or think more about specific trees (Trope and Liberman, 2010).

Managers can frame prosocial messages along a similar temporal dimension as described in CLT. For instance, a firm can present the same societal benefit in future terms like "*supporting the future of our community by investing in elementary school programs*" or, in present terms, by saying "*playing a role in making children's lives better every day by investing in elementary school programs.*" Such temporal orientation has a unique effect on social impact messages, owing to their potential to induce an abstract mindset. Studies find societal messages are more effective in influencing consumer perceptions of a brand when the information is processed via high-level (vs. low-level) construal conditions. For instance, studies have shown that consumers in a low-level construal mindset prefer products that offer more tangible and personal benefits (Meyvis, Goldsmith, and Dhar, 2012[8]); however, consumers in high-level construal mindsets prefer products that have benefits meeting higher-order goals (Dhar and Kim, 2007[9]). Researchers find the impact of a societal message on the perception of product performance to be a function of the level of abstraction. Respondents in a high-level (vs. low-level) construal mindset condition reacted more positively to social goodwill messages (Chernev and Blair, 2015[10]). These results have led researchers to argue that a high-level construal mindset—which focuses attention on higher-order goals (e.g. social impact)—will cause consumers to be further persuaded by appeals for products that promise to benefit the greater good (Goldsmith and Dhar, 2009[11]). Researchers have found other message forms congruent with high- vs. low-level construal to experience similar processing fluency benefits. For instance, studies show that loss frames are more efficacious when paired with low-level construal mindsets, whereas gain frames are more effective when paired with high-level construal mindsets (White, MacDonnell, and Dahl, 2011[12]). Similarly, studies on consumer attitudes and purchase intention resulting from green advertising, find that congruency between gain frames and high-level construal leads to greater processing efficiencies and higher levels of message appeal and persuasion (Chang, Zhang, and Xie, 2015[13]; Lee and Aaker, 2004[14]). A similar congruency effect occurs when changing the beneficiaries of social impact messages from a "benefits to self" to "benefit to others" perspective; consumers could perceive "benefits to self" as more concrete, as these benefits are more psychologically proximal (Goldsmith and Dhar, 2009). As a result, they would be associated with lower-level goal attainment. Conversely, "benefits to others" are more abstract; they are associated with higher-order goals, which are conditions associated with high-level construal.

Our own research finds that social impact messages framed in ways that induce a higher-level construal will generate increased consumer engagement. In particular, three message-framing options—gains (vs. loss), abstract (vs. concrete), and others (vs. self)—all moderate the effect of social impact messages on consumer engagement. The evidence for these effects comes from data we collected on the content of posts and the number of likes and shares for 11,138 social media messages posted on X (formerly Twitter) and Facebook for dozens of brands. Each post was classified as a social impact message if it contained one of three types of social dimensions: environmental, animal, or community well-being. These categories were derived from topics included in the CSR/Sustainability reports by firms in our sample. As illustrated in Figures 8.1 and 8.2, we find that stimulating attitudinal engagement with social impact brand messages requires content to be framed in more future (vs. present) terms, a focus on solutions (vs. problems) and benefits to "others" (vs. the "self").

In this chapter, we discussed five principles that managers can use to guide the development of social impact messages that work, while at the same time reducing some of the risks associated with the pursuit of good growth. It starts with ensuring authenticity by prioritizing consistency with past behaviors and aligning societal benefits with product benefits or brand associations. Instead of creating a traditional ad campaign, brands should consider actionable interventions that demonstrate commitment and pay particular attention to the planning of audiences, as well as placement and timing of messages. Keep in mind too, that consumers are skeptical about brands' motives when it comes to social impact. Providing evidence of sincerity, like a fit between the brand and the societal issue, minimizing the product's role in the message, and providing concrete benefits can be a principal factor in driving acceptance. Finally, the framing of messages is crucial. Using high-level construal (abstract and future-oriented) rather than low-level construal (concrete and present-oriented) can enhance consumers' involvement and engagement with your efforts.

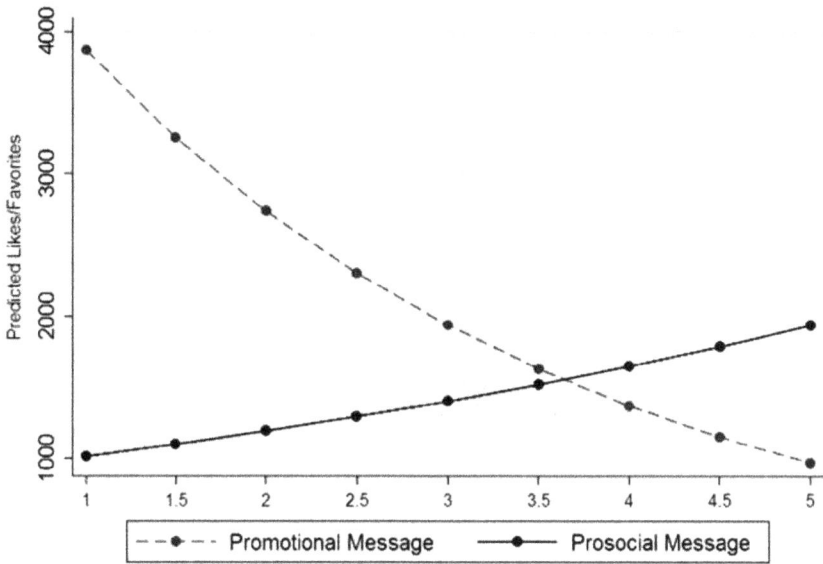

Figure 8.1 Problem vs. Solution Framing.

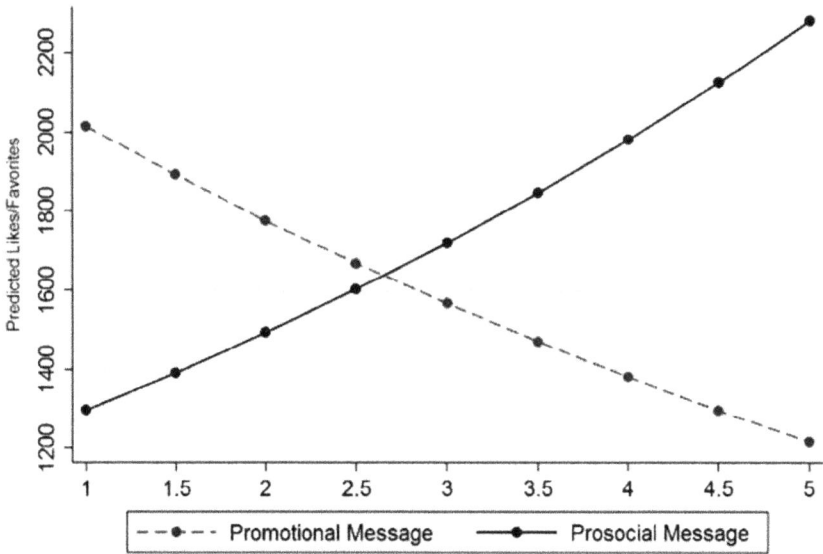

Figure 8.2 Present vs. Future Framing.

Notes

1 Lee, D., Hosanagar, K., & Nair, H. S. (2018). Advertising content and consumer engagement on social media: Evidence from Facebook. *Management Science, 64* (11), 5105–5131.
2 Malhotra, A., Malhotra, C. K., & See, A. (2013). How to create brand engagement on Facebook. *MIT Sloan Management Review, 54*(2).
3 Schamp, C., Heitmann, M., Bijmolt, T. H., & Katzenstein, R. (2023). The effectiveness of cause-related marketing: A meta-analysis on consumer responses. *Journal of Marketing Research*, 60(1), 189–215.
4 Dubé, J.-P., Luo, X., & Fang, Z. (2017). Self-signaling and prosocial behavior: A cause marketing experiment. *Marketing Science, 36*(2), 161–186.
5 Arora, N. & Henderson, T. (2007). Embedded premium promotion: Why it works and how to make it more effective. *Marketing Science, 26*(4), 514–531.
6 *Chicago Booth Review*. (2020, September 15). Corporate responses to Black Lives Matter: Commitment speaks volumes. Chicago Booth.
7 Trope, Y. & Liberman, N. (2010). Construal-level theory of psychological distance. *Psychological Review, 117*(2), 440–463.
8 Meyvis, T., Goldsmith, K., & Dhar, R. (2012). The importance of the context in brand extension: How pictures and comparisons shift consumers' focus from fit to quality. *Journal of Marketing Research, 49*(2), 206–217.
9 Dhar, R. & Kim, E. Y. (2007). Seeing the forest or the trees: Implications of construal level theory for consumer choice. *Journal of Consumer Psychology, 17* (2), 96–100.
10 Chernev, A. & Blair, S. (2015). Doing well by doing good: The benevolent halo of corporate social responsibility. *Journal of Consumer Research, 41*(6), 1412–1425.
11 Goldsmith, K. & Dhar, R. (2009). The Role of Abstract and Concrete Mindsets on the Purchase of Adjacent Products. *Advances in Consumer Research, 36*, 37–40.
12 White, K., MacDonnell, R., & Dahl, D. W. (2011). It's the mind-set that matters: The role of construal level and message framing in influencing consumer efficacy and conservation behaviors. *Journal of Marketing Research, 48*(3), 472–485
13 Chang, H., Zhang, L., & Xie, G. X. (2015). Message framing in green advertising: The effect of construal level and consumer environmental concern. *International Journal of Advertising, 34*(1), 158–176.
14 Lee, A. Y. & Aaker, J. L. (2004). Bringing the frame into focus: The influence of regulatory fit on processing fluency and persuasion. *Journal of Personality and Social Psychology, 86*(2), 205–218.

Chapter 9

Assessing the Impact

A well-known business adage says that what gets measured gets managed, and social impact efforts are no exception. Seeking to create societal benefits for customers without a follow-up measurement or program evaluation plan is likely to lead to a short-lived program. Just as important, measurement is also needed to enable managers to improve the performance of the program over time. Yet, one of the most difficult aspects of competing on social impact is measuring the contribution of those investments on both the societal and business needs. As part of our work over the last ten years into the management of good growth, we have crafted four principles that can facilitate this important task for managers.

Measure Consequences, Not Just Results

Most marketing managers think of measurement in relation to the return on marketing investment in their brand or business. Did the effort result in a desired sales increase, help grow the customer base, or expand market share? The results measured in marketing are many and vary greatly by brand and industry. One important distinction with managers that are competing on social impact is that they go beyond measuring results, to also measuring the consequences of their programs on the societal need. For instance, Lifebuoy is a low-cost hand soap offering by Unilever which is sold in many countries around the world. While it first launched in 1894, it gradually disappeared from several Western countries including the US. Its global market share dropped from 11.2 percent in 2005 to 9.7 percent in 2009 and in India, the largest Lifebuoy market, the share of market decreased from 18.4 percent to 15.5 percent in the same period. To revitalize the business, the brand managers decided to incorporate a societal benefit as part of the positioning of the brand. In India, the brand had a legacy association with hygiene and health, owing partly to a jingle that ads made popular in 1964—'*Tandurusti ki raksha karta hai Lifebuoy, Lifebuoy hai jahan tandurusti hai wahan*'—which meant "*Lifebuoy protects health, Lifebuoy is there where there is health.*" In 2010 Lifebuoy partnered with global

DOI: 10.4324/9781003383246-10

organizations such as UNICEF, state and local governments, and local NGOs to enhance sanitation practices in an effort they named "Help a child reach 5" intended to significantly reduce childhood mortality, owing to waterborne illnesses that can be prevented with better hand washing habits. They also added to their list of partners a different type of stakeholder— academic institutions. Their role was to evaluate outcomes not on the business, but on the societal goal of reducing childhood mortality. Encouraging hand washing for personal hygiene is a challenging public health goal that requires significant efforts to help change day-to-day behaviors, not only on the part of the consumer but also on the available infrastructure in schools or homes. An evaluation of a water, sanitation, and hygiene (WASH) program showed that the percent of respondents who were aware of the importance of the behavior and practiced the behavior—also called the knowledge-behavior gap—was smaller (85 percent) than the gap in the treatment of drinking water (49 percent) and sanitation (37 percent)[1]. The challenge of personal hygiene that the brand assumed called for a more systematic evaluation.

While the brand was focused on schools, they systematically evaluated the impact with a randomized control design study using a sample of children and their mothers in a slum in Mumbai. The study in 70 low-income communities in Mumbai, involved researchers measuring soap consumption as a proxy for handwashing and its outcomes in terms of illnesses, including diarrhea and acute respiratory infections (ARIs), as well as school absences for 41 weeks. The results indicated that hand washing reduced episodes of diarrhea and ARIs for target five-year-olds and their families by 25 percent. There were also 27 percent fewer absences from school, due to illness for the five-year-olds. Additional analyses suggest that the intervention also reduced eye infections among the same age group[2]. Furthermore, in collaboration with the academic partners, the brand team ran a shorter program over the course of three weeks in the state of Bihar in India. They designed the intervention as a similar randomized control trial and found no evidence of the health-relevant effects they were hoping to achieve via hand washing with Lifebuoy soap in schoolchildren and their mothers. This helped the team learn where their program was falling short, in particular the limited campaign intensity, ineffective delivery, and lack of comprehension of the challenging physical and social environments[3].

Lifebuoy also designed programs in Kenya in partnership with Sightsavers, a non-governmental organization working on a mission to expand hand and face washing habits in emerging countries. The work reached more than 200,000 children. Teachers in 116 schools were encouraged to champion the program. The effort reduced preventable trachoma (blindness) by 30 percent and the program has since expanded to Ethiopia and Zambia. Largely focused on school children through teachers and mothers, these programs have not only increased sales for the firm but have also impacted societal goals. Both these illustrations involved using a controlled field experiment to evaluate the outcomes, thus increasing confidence in the results.

Broadening the measurement scope to include not only business results but social outcomes increases support from non-commercial stakeholders such as NGOs and government officials, enhancing the credibility and in some cases reducing the cost of social impact initiatives as partners are compelled to share resources. Unilever Ltd India and the Children's Investment Fund Foundation (CIFF) funded the handwashing campaign in India. CIFF paid for the outcome evaluation because the results were in line with their mission. From the brand's perspective, in 2015 Lifebuoy held the fourth-place ranking in Kantar Worldpanel valuation of users and buying frequency among 11,000 brands in 35 countries. By 2022, when newly renamed Kantar Brand Footprint study[4] was extended to 53 countries and 37,000 brands, Lifebuoy still held the #6 position worldwide among the most chosen consumer-packaged goods brands. The branding expert David Aaker captured a good summary of its success.[5]:

> In my view, there are three reasons why this program stands out. First, it attacks a visible, meaningful, and emotional problem that is relevant to Unilever's core international markets—the life expectancy of infants. And it does so with a concept (handwashing) that has demonstrative value. Second, the design and execution of the program is creative and effective. Kids and moms are taught and motivated to wash "the right way," using a wide variety of tools and methods. Third, the program is intricately tied to Lifebuoy as hand washing suggests the use of Lifebuoy soap. Further, the linkage draws on Lifebuoy's heritage as a disease-fighting soap product. Although other organizations are also active in the handwashing movement, Lifebuoy, for many, has become the exemplar.

Earlier in the book we discussed the Dove case, which is also an example of a brand that measured consequences, not just results. Similarly to Lifebuoy, academic partners used randomized controlled trials to understand the effect of the brand's efforts on the self-esteem of girls exposed to the program. The results found a positive impact by the alternative approaches used, such as one- hour and multi-hour programs in schools, feedback from their partner organizations, and YouTube videos. The findings were critical as the partners, including universities, the UN, and the World Association of Girl Guides and Scouts, would not have endorsed the program without evidence of effectiveness.

Measure the Negative Not Just the Positive

It is common for managers to track consumer perception of their brands, yet in most cases, the measurement focuses on positive associations. For instance, how many people like the product, are willing to buy it, or associate it with superior quality or affordable prices? However, as discussed in Chapter 8, social impact strategies can provoke passionate reactions by customers which at times, can be critical or negative towards the brand as we discussed earlier. Therefore, it is important for managers to include metrics and signals in their brand measures that can assess negative perceptions towards the brand or negative consequences of their social impact actions. This is particularly relevant in social media dominated environments which consumers use to share both positive and negative reactions to a brand's social impact work. For example, in September 2018, when Nike utilized Colin Kaepernick in its "Dream Crazy" ad for the 30th anniversary of the Just Do It campaign, the reaction was swift. Within 24 hours the ad received 80 million views on social media. One in five reactions were negative, yet capturing both positive and negative sentiments provided a deeper understanding of its impact. While 21 percent of respondents reported a lower likelihood of buying, thus representing a type of boycott of Nike's products, 29 percent expressed a greater purchase intent. Moreover, online sales for the week of the ad grew 31 percent, compared to 17 percent for the same period the previous year. The reactions among African American and Hispanic consumers were significantly more positive in terms of purchase likelihood and engagement, while the Caucasian consumers were more negative on both counts. Further, Nike noted that the negative reactions were among people aged 45 or older, while millennials and Gen X consumers showed a positive reaction. While Nike was an all-age group brand, the younger consumer base bought disproportionately more shoes and other Nike-branded products. Scott Galloway, another marketing expert, provided a good back of the envelope calculation examining both the positive and negative effects:

> Nike registers $35 billion in revenues—$15 billion domestically and $20B abroad. Two-thirds of Nike consumers are under the age of 35. A younger consumer who can afford $150 Flyknit racers likely has substantial disposable income and lives in a city. The term for this cohort? Progressive. Of the $20B international customer base, how many believe the US is currently a "beacon on a hill" and is handling race issues well? Nike has risked $1–3B in business to strengthen their relationship with consumers who account for $32–34B of their franchise. The math? Nike just did it.

Firms can also learn from negative sentiment and take quick corrective action like Netflix did following their messages of support for the Black

Lives Matter movement. Provoked by the murder of George Floyd and the civil unrest that followed, Netflix made two supportive statements on social media regarding Black Lives Matter. Perhaps, because they were perceived as words only, they did not evoke much of a net reaction and resulting in a decrease in both positive and negative sentiment. Following up, Netflix offered a third statement pledging $5 million of support to Black Lives Matter (BLM) organizations. In a potentially unexpected reaction, researchers[6] found that their initial donation statement faced a 61 percent increase in negative sentiment indicating that the firm's commitment to the cause was underwhelming. Netflix subsequently issued a fourth statement pledging an increased amount of $120 million. The negative sentiment subsided while the positive sentiment remained high. Ensuring that the monitoring systems of a brand incorporate negative signals will enable managers to adjust their social impact programs more rapidly and avoid the type of large-scale consumer response that have, at times, created reputational or business damage to brands.

Measure Response Across Stakeholders

As the Scott Galloway analysis discussed earlier shows, while consumer reactions and demand are important to monitor, firms involved in social impact actions also need to keep track of other stakeholder reactions. Clearly, investors are critical stakeholders, especially for publicly traded firms. Academic research[7] finds that on average, shareholders in the stock market view firm actions on social and environmental issues negatively. However, a deeper dive suggests that it varies by how far the firms deviate from stakeholders' values and the brand's image. Ron Johnson, who came to JCPenney as CEO from Apple Inc., launched same-sex partner ads on Father's Day and Mother's Day. Stakeholders reacted negatively, and the stock price went into a free fall, which contributed to Johnson's exit. While these ads may have been appropriate for other brands, they deviated significantly from JCPenney's more conservative culture.

In our research[8], we examined the effect of firms launching products with social benefits and its effect on investor response. We utilized a direct revealed measure of investor attention to the launch announcements of new products with social benefits. Efficient market theory suggests that information about firms is instantaneously incorporated into stock prices. So, investors' attention is an important metric, especially since their attention is a scarce cognitive resource. A news article in the Wall Street Journal does not guarantee attention unless investors read or hear about it. This is especially true where we have "a wealth of information that creates a poverty of attention". To address this, we utilize Google's search volume index, because it differs from existing proxies of investor attention, captures investor attention in a timelier manner, and measures the attention of a broader set of investors.

We find that investor attention is consistently higher during the five-day window before and after the launch of social benefit products. For companies that have only social benefit product introductions (as opposed to a portfolio mixed with regular products), the investor attention gradually increases, peaking on the day of the launch while slowly regressing towards the mean. This is similar to the case of firms with new products that carry social benefits. However, for firms with new products that include environmental benefits, the search volume continues to rise past the launch date. This signals that the environmental benefit is long-term oriented but less tangible, concrete, and relevant to investors. Overall, firms with new products that carry social benefits, in comparison to their counterpart firms launching new products without social benefits, show higher levels of investor attention that should predict higher stock prices.

Employees are also critical stakeholders to manage as part of social impact programs[9]. Brands' societal benefits can help hire and retain high-quality talent, especially among Millennial and Gen Z age groups. Tracking their reactions to the brand's positions can help in this regard. Starbucks perceived lukewarm support of BLM and its employees viewed the policy of prohibiting them from wearing BLM-related clothing in stores as hypocritical and endangering employee engagement. This eventually forced the company to not only change its policy, but also commit to making 250,000 Black Lives Matter shirts for baristas who wanted them. In addition to listening to social media, firms can use employee engagement surveys or investor sentiment assessments to track reactions across different stakeholders for their social impact initiatives.

Finally, it is also important to measure the impact of a social impact strategy on the NGO or community partners and their population of donors or volunteers. Coca-Cola did just that when partnering with the WWF on their Arctic Home program. They worked together with WWF managers to survey their donors and volunteer communities to assess their response to the partnership. The feedback was mainly positive, but the effort helped WWF identify segments of the donor community that expressed concerns about their partnership and the potential commercialization of the WWF mission. Identifying those issues helped WWF managers mitigate a potential reputational risk with this essential stakeholder group.

Measure Effect on Demand

Not measuring the impact of social impact initiatives on demand could lead to serious underfunding. In turn, the lack of funding may hurt the brand's performance essentially creating a vicious cycle. A classic illustration of this phenomenon was the Campaign for Real Beauty (CFRB) for the Dove brand which we discussed earlier in the book. Dove supplemented the CFRB media campaign with the Dove Self-Esteem Project in which the brand managers collaborated with academic professionals to create research-driven programs aimed at fostering positive body image among millions of teenagers world-wide. Campaigns further supported this initiative by advocating for policies limiting image retouching in ads, referred to as "Brand Do". These efforts involved independent academic research, including randomized controlled trials, which validated that the Dove Self-Esteem Project initiatives effectively enhanced self-esteem and body confidence. Nevertheless, regional brand managers initially hesitated to reallocate funds from direct product marketing to the program. Country brand managers were the ultimate decision-makers on how their marketing budget was to be allocated given that they were also responsible for delivering on the financial goals for the brand. One key concern was that the Campaign for Real Beauty advertising did not feature Dove products. Country brand managers feared that the brand communication would not reach target consumers and was less suited to emerging markets, which were the fastest growing market for Dove sales. However, measuring the impact on demand showed that awareness of the Campaign for Real Beauty and the Dove Self-Esteem Project increased their purchase intent by 10 percent to 25 percent—a significant increase, according to company officials. Additional research showed that the regions with the highest spending on both social impact efforts had the strongest sales growth. The Campaign for Real Beauty won numerous awards and gained extraordinary media attention generating an exceptional return on investment ($4.42 for every dollar spent) compared to typical marketing campaigns. Evidence of the impact on consumer demand helped persuade country brand managers to invest in the initiative.

Consumer response to social benefits in product offerings is difficult to measure. As we alluded to early in the book, a primary reason is the gap between stated intentions and actual behavior of people. In survey after survey, consumers state that they prefer to purchase products that offer social benefits over products that do not by a significant margin. Moreover, they often state that they are willing to pay a premium for such products. However, conversations with managers suggest that these behaviors from consumers are unlikely based on their experience. This has two potential consequences. First, the managers' perceptions are accurate and therefore consumers' intentions are overstated. Second, managers' views are incorrect, and consumers' intentions are undervalued. Both explanations call for better measurement of consumer demand and willingness to pay instead of relying solely on consumer perceptual surveys. While consumer surveys are useful for descriptive purposes, they often suffer from social desirability bias. Social desirability bias occurs when respondents in a survey provide answers they believe are more socially acceptable or favorable, rather than their true thoughts or behaviors. In a business context, this bias can lead to inaccurate data, as respondents might overstate positive intentions or underreport

negative ones to appear more favorable to others. The bias could be particularly acute in the case of responses towards societal benefits in products.
Based on our research and those of others, we introduce a few options to
consider below that help overcome this bias and provide better measures of
consumer response to social benefit offerings.

Choice-based conjoint (CBC) analysis

This is a popular market research technique used to understand customer preferences and the value consumers place on different features of a product or
service. CBC presents respondents with a set of choices that mimic real-world
purchasing decisions. This approach provides more realistic data on how consumers make trade-offs among different product features and benefits. For
example, when evaluating preferences for smartphones, respondents might be
shown different combinations of brand, price, battery life, and camera quality
and asked to choose their preferred option. As we present our research later,
one could add to this list of attributes, a societal attribute such as raw materials
from fair trade practices or conflict-free countries for some options and not
others to see the differential impact on the consumers' choice. CBC helps
determine how consumers value different attributes and what trade-offs they
are willing to make. It quantifies the relative importance of each attribute in the
decision-making process. In the example above, CBC can determine how much
consumers are willing to pay for social benefits and calculate their relative
importance vs. other more functional benefits. By understanding how different
attributes influence choices, CBC can help in predicting market share for various product configurations and simulate demand under different market scenarios. For example, by adding social benefits to the product offer, CBC can
help estimate the incremental market share, if any, as a result of the change.
Researchers can customize CBC to study a wide range of products and services
with various attributes and levels. This flexibility allows it to be tailored to
specific research questions and markets. Marketers can apply CBC to consumer
goods, services, healthcare plans, or even public policies, making it versatile for
different research needs. Particularly useful to marketers, CBC can provide
detailed information on consumer preferences at an individual level.
Companies can use this rich data for segmentation and targeting specific
customer groups with tailored offerings. For instance, a company can
identify segments that value sustainability highly and target them with
eco-friendly product options. CBC is well-suited for studying products
with multiple attributes and levels, even when the choice sets are complex. It simplifies the analysis of how different attribute combinations
affect preferences. When studying preferences for a new health insurance
plan, CBC can handle various features such as coverage options, premiums, deductibles, and provider networks. Additionally, it can combine
product and service features as well as intangibles such as brands.

Using CBC, a company developing an eco-friendly product could present different product profiles, each with varying combinations of environmental attributes (e.g. recyclable materials, low carbon footprint, energy efficiency), and ask respondents to choose their preferred option. This approach would provide insights into how consumers value different combinations of attributes and the trade-offs they are willing to make, helping the company design a product that maximizes consumer appeal while meeting environmental goals.

CBC is useful in a variety of contexts. For example, when developing a new product or service, CBC can help identify the optimal combination of features and attributes that will appeal to target customers. A tech company designing a new laptop can use CBC to understand the preferred balance between performance, battery life, weight, and price. CBC is also useful for determining the best pricing strategy by assessing how price changes impact consumer choices and the perceived value of other attributes. An airline can use CBC to determine how changes in ticket prices, baggage fees, seat comfort, and carbon fees affect consumer preferences and booking decisions. As mentioned earlier, CBC can help identify distinct customer segments based on their preferences and the trade-offs they are willing to make. This aids in targeted marketing and product positioning. A car manufacturer can use CBC to segment the market based on preferences for features like fuel efficiency, safety, luxury, and price and then tailor marketing campaigns for each segment. When evaluating competitive positioning, CBC can provide insights into how a product or service compares to competitors based on consumer preferences for different attributes. An illustration would be a detergent manufacturer using CBC to analyze how its new green detergent stacks up against competitors in terms of features, price, and brand perception. It could also analyze where its new growth is coming from, whether from competitors, cannibalization, or completely new customers. Finally, CBC can assess the impact of policy changes or new regulations on consumer choices and market dynamics. For example, a government agency can use CBC to understand how different policy scenarios (e.g. subsidies for electric vehicles) might influence consumer adoption rates. In summary, choice-based conjoint analysis is a powerful tool for understanding consumer preferences and making informed decisions about product development, pricing, market segmentation, and competitive strategy. Its ability to mirror real-world choices and provide detailed insights into attribute trade-offs makes it invaluable for market researchers and businesses seeking to optimize their offerings and strategies. It directs people closer to their true preferences by overcoming social desirability bias[10] and making respondents choose among tradeoffs through an indirect approach to estimating preferences for attributes and pricing based on choices, not opinions.

We start with an illustration of a simple study we conducted with our students. First, using a survey-based approach, we asked them about their preference for several products made with recycled plastic. Among the top choices were T-shirts. We next conducted a conjoint type of analysis, where we forced them to make tradeoffs between different features, including the use of recycled plastic in the product options. Based on this analysis, T-shirts with recycled plastic ended up as 28th among 30 choices. This study illustrates the differences between opinions that are prone to social desirability and utilizes an indirect approach to get closer to real preferences.

We[11] also conducted consumer experiments using a choice-based conjoint (CBC) analysis to examine consumer preferences, purchase intent, and willingness to pay (WTP) for sustainable benefit claims while controlling for other product attributes (e.g. brand, flavor, price, etc.). We treated the health/performance attributes as necessary or as a table stakes dimension. Using a sample of 1,000 respondents from a U.S. online panel, we chose two categories: i) Greek yogurt to represent the food category; and ii) skin lotion for non-food. For the yogurt category, we included a recyclable cup, product from pasture raised cows, a certification by the Rainforest Alliance as environmental features and a Feed America contribution as social benefits in the CBC study. For the skin lotion category study, we used biodegradable packaging, no petrochemicals in the product as environmental features, no animal testing and a contribution to skin cancer research as social benefit features in the CBC experiment. We found that the environmental and societal attributes had higher utility in the purchase decision than healthy attributes in the yogurt study. They ranged from 3 percent to nearly 17 percent, with only flavor and brand name having greater utility. In the skin lotion category, apart from scent, animal testing was highly valued in the decision-making process and dominated other attributes such as brand, skin type, and even price. Concerning willingness to pay for the lotion and yogurt categories, the results indicate that social attributes had the highest WTP, followed by environmental attributes. For the average yogurt cup priced at $1.29, the study participants were willing to pay between $0.22–$0.29 incremental premium for the environmental and social features of the product, amounting to nearly 20 percent–25 percent premium. For the skincare category, for a pack size that sold at $11.99, the study participants were willing to pay a $3.22 premium for a product with no animal testing. This amounted to a 27 percent premium over a product without that promise.

We have conducted similar studies with other categories such as shoes, sandwiches, laptops, ride share and laundry detergents. Across these studies, we found that the CBC analysis helps us to examine the customer preference and price premiums that consumers are willing to pay for sustainable products.

Max Diff Method

Another research approach to understand the utility of social impact on customers is Max Diff, short for Maximum Difference scaling, which is a survey-based technique used to measure preferences or the importance of different features or benefits of products. Researchers present respondents with sets of items and ask them to indicate the most and least important item in each set. The goal is to identify the relative importance or preference of each item. For example, a company wants to develop an eco-friendly product and needs to determine which environmental attributes (e.g. recyclable materials, low carbon footprint, energy efficiency) are most important to consumers. Using Max Diff, the company can present these attributes in sets and ask respondents to select the most and least important ones. The results will help prioritize which features to focus on in product development and marketing. It is a useful method to distinguish between options because it forces respondents to make clear choices. The task is straightforward, as respondents only need to pick the best and worst options. It provides a clear numerical ranking of items based on preference or importance while requiring fewer questions than other ranking methods to achieve reliable results. It is useful in several marketing contexts, including product feature prioritization in product development and feature promotion choices, such as identifying the most important environmental or societal attributes to include in a product.

As discussed earlier, to draw a direct comparison with CBC, Max Diff is simpler for respondents and provides clear prioritization, while CBC offers more detailed insights into consumer preferences and trade-offs. Second, Max Diff typically requires fewer questions, making it less burdensome for respondents compared to CBC, which may need a more extended survey to cover all combinations. Third, Max Diff is ideal for prioritizing attributes or items because it enables managers to test the relative importance across dozens of options, whereas CBC is better suited for understanding the relative value of a handful of attributes, typically not more than five or six. It is important to recognize that as a researcher seeking to measure the importance and value of social benefits, Max Diff is a valuable tool for prioritizing items or attributes efficiently and clearly, making it ideal for the initial stages of a social impact strategy or when quick insights are needed. In contrast, CBC provides a deeper understanding of consumer preferences and trade-offs, which is useful for detailed product design and assessing market share impacts. Context matters when making a choice between the two. Use Max Diff for straightforward prioritization tasks and CBC for complex decision-making scenarios where understanding trade-offs is crucial. By leveraging these tools appropriately, managers can make more informed decisions, align product features with consumer values, and ultimately enhance product success in the market.

Other Approaches

While using CBC and Max Diff approaches are probably the best ways to address social desirability bias, if firms are constrained to using a survey-based approach, we list simpler actions below that firms can take to mitigate social desirability bias.

1 *Assure Anonymity and Confidentiality.* In survey-based studies about preferences for eco-friendly products, start with a statement like, "Your responses are completely anonymous and confidential. We appreciate your honest feedback."

2 *Use Indirect Questioning Techniques.* Two approaches are available here. First, use a Third-Person Technique. For example, in a survey, ask, "How do you think your friends feel about buying from brands that support social causes?". Another approach, especially useful when respondents perceive the issue as sensitive and are unwilling to talk about it, is a projective technique. In the case of research on products with social benefits, the researcher could show a picture of a product with an eco-friendly label and ask, "What kind of person do you think buys this product?" This frees up the respondent from talking about their choice mitigating social desirability.

3 *Randomized Response Technique.* This involves using a random number generator to determine if the respondent should answer a sensitive question directly or answer a different, less sensitive question. For instance, "If your number is even, answer whether you prefer eco-friendly brands. If odd, answer whether you prefer brands with high discounts." While it might call for a large sample, it has the potential to mitigate bias in response.

4 *Include Neutral Wording.* In your survey, instead of asking, "Do you prefer products that are eco-friendly?" ask, "What factors are important to you when choosing a product?"

5 *Use Validated Scales.* This is a method often used in academic research. Here, as a part of the survey, researchers incorporate items from the Marlowe-Crowne Social Desirability Scale. This helps to identify respondents who may be giving socially desirable answers. This can help to account for bias in the analysis phase.

6 *Conducting Anonymous Online Surveys.* This involves using an online survey platform to ask questions about preferences for socially responsible brands. As part of the introduction, highlight the anonymity of the responses to encourage honesty.

Using Behavioral Measures

In a distinct approach from survey research, instead of asking customers if they would buy a product with a societal benefit, track their actual purchases or engagement with it. We reviewed results from this approach earlier in the book when providing evidence of social impact's effect on business. It can be particularly effective when trying to understand the viability of market demand for social impact in a specific category. Researchers have used this approach to study the relationship between social impact and various aspects of business performance. A recent study[12] using granular barcode-level sales data from Nielsen's panel of U.S. retail stores finds that one standard deviation (0.10) increase in environmental and social (E&S) ratings increases sales by 9.2 percent. Thus, when a firm has a better E&S performance, as reflected by third-party ratings, there is a higher consumer demand for the firm's products. However, they do not find that better E&S ratings lead to higher product unit prices. Thus, a better firm E&S profile contributes to higher revenues primarily through higher consumer demand for the product. Utilizing behavioral data also helps identify consumer segments that are more prone to purchasing products with social impact. The research finds that the positive effect is greater in counties with more Democratic-leaning households. Effectively, a one standard deviation increase (0.14) in Democratic households leads to an 8.5 percent increase in sales for products with better E&S ratings. The effect of E&S ratings on product sales is stronger for higher-income households, with a one standard deviation (10.8) increase in per capita income leading to a 5.9 percent increase in sales. Better performance by competitors on the ESG ratings reduced the firm's sales, suggesting the presence of competitive effects. Having access to rich behavioral data can also help firms identify the role of context. Negative news about a firm's E&S issues hurts the firm's sales of E&S products. Interestingly, immediately after major natural and environmental disasters, sales in counties close to the disasters become more sensitive to E&S ratings. This finding provides insights into when social benefits needs can be promoted for enhanced impact.

In conclusion, when measuring impact, it is important to acknowledge that research in the business environment has traditionally relied on correlational studies to draw insights for decision-making. While correlations are necessary for causation, they are not sufficient. Correlations could be spurious and lead to incorrect insights that become the basis for wasteful spending. Earlier in this chapter, we discussed the use of randomized control design studies by Unilever to causally determine the public health benefits of handwashing. This methodology is the gold standard in determining causality. While experiments are ideal, they are difficult to execute in the real world. The emergence of Large Language models and Generative AI such as ChatGPT has made it possible for firms to utilize synthetic subjects for experimental studies. The GenAI environment is a relatively inexpensive and quick way to conduct research and represents the future of market research in many areas.

What gets measured gets managed. But at the same time, that familiar saying can constrain managers in their pursuit of growth by only allowing them to take actions that can be measured. Therefore, it is important to use the methods described above to also think innovatively about how to measure the impact and return of social impact investments in new ways, opening the possibility for greater innovation.

Notes

1 Schlegelmilch, M. P., Lakhani, A., Saunders, L. D., & Jhangri, G. S. (2016). Evaluation of water, sanitation and hygiene program outcomes shows knowledge-behavior gaps in Coast Province, Kenya. *Pan African Medical Journal,* 23: 145.
2 Nicholson, J. A., Naeeni, M., Hoptroff, M., Matheson, J. R., Roberts, A. J., Taylor, D., Sidibe, M., Weir, A. J., Damle, S. G., & Wright, R. L. (2014). An investigation of the effects of a hand washing intervention on health outcomes and school absence using a randomized trial in Indian urban communities. *Tropical Medicine & International Health,* 19(3): 284–292.
3 Lewis, H. E., Greenland, K., Curtis, V., & Schmidt, W. P. (2018). Effect of a school-based hygiene behavior change campaign on handwashing with soap in Bihar, India: Cluster-randomized trial. *American Journal of Tropical Medicine and Hygiene,* 99(4): 924–933.
4 Kantar (2023). *Brand footprint 2023.* Kantar.
5 Prophet (2015, October 7). *Lifebuoy: The best social responsibility program ever?* Prophet.
6 Chintagunta, P. K., Kansal, Y., & Pachigolla, P. (2020). In corporate responses to Black Lives Matter, commitment speaks volumes. *Chicago Booth Review.*
7 Bhagwat, Y., Warren, N. L., Beck, J. T., & Watson IV, G. F. (2020). Corporate sociopolitical activism and firm value. *Journal of Marketing,* 84(5): 1–21.
8 Kim, Y. & Bharadwaj, S. (2023). Environmental and social claims in new products and financial performance. Working Paper, University of Tennessee.
9 Creswell, J. & Yaffe-Bellany, D. (2020, June 12). Starbucks, reversing itself, will allow workers to wear Black Lives Matter attire. *The New York Times.*
10 Horiuchi, Y., Markovich, Z., & Yamamoto, T. (2022). Does conjoint analysis mitigate social desirability bias? *Political Analysis,* 30(4): 535–549.
11 Kim, Y. & Bharadwaj, S. (n.d.). Environmental and social claims in new products and financial performance. Working Paper, University of Tennessee.
12 Meier, I., Servaes, H., Wei, J., & Xiao, Y. (2023). Do consumers care about ESG? Evidence from barcode-level sales data. *SSRN.*

Chapter 10

Managing the Risks of Social Impact Work

The video of their new product began to circulate on social media a few weeks before Earth Day. With a song by Marc Robillard in the background and the image of a flower growing, Sunchips introduced the first biodegradable bag of chips in the USA market. This launch was a reminder of the increasing concerns over pollution driven by plastic bags. According to the Environmental Protection Agency (EPA)[1], in 2018 the U.S. generated 4.2 million tons of plastic bags, sacks, and wraps, of which only 10 percent was recycled. Separately, the Center for Biological Diversity reports that the average American family uses 1,500 plastic bags annually, equating to about four bags per day. With approximately 128 million households in the U.S., this totals over 500 million plastic bags used daily. Given this reality, the new package was celebrated by many environmental groups and opinion leaders as an example for others to follow. However, the product was taken off supermarket shelves two months after its introduction, following an outcry from consumers. The concern was not about the safety of the bags or how they may change the taste of the product. In fact, the problem that turned this well-intended and much-celebrated innovation into a commercial failure was an unexpected issue that few saw coming...its noise. Videos of people, many of them college students, began to circulate on social media sites featuring different memes or complaints about the loud noise the bag made when being opened or when holding it. We might think that the bag's noise is a small price to pay for the reduction in plastic, but the experience left the Frito Lays team with a hard lesson—most consumers will put their personal utility ahead of many societal ones. What started as a major sign of progress in the journey of many marketers to turn social impact into an advantage became a symbol of its risk and challenges. It is not uncommon for new products or services to fail. In fact, most new products fail to reach commercial levels that enable their presence in the market for more than a few years. Therefore, the conclusion from the Sunchips experience should not be that social impact is risky and, therefore, not worth the effort. Instead, the conclusion is that competing on social impact is a form of innovation with similar levels of risks and benefits. In this chapter, we will discuss some of the

DOI: 10.4324/9781003383246-11

most common and predictable challenges that social impact programs face and how to avoid them in order to strengthen their chances of success.

Translating social to commercial value, like many other forms of innovation, can be difficult. Many well-intended initiatives such as the Sunchips biodegradable bag, the Starbucks "race together" program, the launch of the GreenWorks brand of cleaners, and the Pepsi Refresh project yielded disappointing results and social media criticism, which caused executives to reconsider their potential as a growth driver. However, in many circumstances, the causes of the negative outcomes can be mitigated.

Negative Associations

Marketers are trained to understand the needs of consumers and identify benefits that would be relevant to their most important needs. However, leaders of good growth efforts need to go beyond relevance to understand the associations that consumers will make about the brand once exposed to its societal benefit. Take, for instance, the benefit claim of "organic" ingredients. If you see it on the label of a tea product or a salad, you may associate it with something that will enhance the product. It will either make it taste better or be of better quality. However, how would you react if the organic product was a pizza? Or a shampoo? A growing body of academic research is showing that consumers don't have an equal or easily predicted response to sustainability claims[2]. Benefits like fair trade, organic, environmentally friendly, or others may be thought of as "good" by marketers, but depending on the category, they may be perceived as "bad" by consumers[3]. To manage the risk of negative associations, it is important for managers to be proactive in understanding the interpretation by different segments of consumers for specific types of societal benefits a brand is considering. Will consumers perceive the claim as an asset? A liability? Or as irrelevant to the purchase? More likely, what percentage of consumers see it as an asset and what percentage as a liability? An example in the household cleaning category illustrates the importance of this step. When launched, GreenWorks represented the first new brand introduction by the Clorox Company in over twenty years and the first mainstream entry by any international consumer-packaged goods company in the growing segment of green household cleaning products. Two years later, the product failed to generate the expected sales, and the initial promise of becoming a dominant player in this more premium market never materialized. One important inhibitor of their success was their selection of claims. Data from Clorox's own consumer research investigating the more important attributes for consumers revealed a problem. While there was expressed interest in environmentally friendly cleaning products, only a small segment of the market, representing 15 percent of sales, perceived it as an important benefit guiding their decision to purchase. In other segments, the presence of environmentally friendly or natural ingredients meant less cleaning efficacy. Clorox brand managers knew of this risk, and they delayed the launch of the products twice until they considered that their formulation was able to deliver the same cleaning power as traditional cleaners. In addition, they decided to include the Clorox logo on the label to reinforce the message of cleaning efficacy. Even the product name GreenWorks is also an intentional step towards reducing the perceived liability by consumers. However, a problem of associations still emerged in the market. First, the most environmentally conscious consumer segment, representing 15 percent of the market, was not attracted to a product so closely associated with the Clorox company, which, represented the type of toxic chemicals many of them did not want in their homes. The other segment of the market interpreted the meaning of a "natural" Clorox product as a less effective Clorox product. In the end, despite a strong launch, the brand was unable to sustain the trial and delivered significantly lower-than-expected results. A change in packaging was subsequently introduced to course correct the initial challenges created by their branding choices. In the new packaging, their main claim of a "natural" cleaner was changed to an "all-purpose" cleaner. A message of "powerful cleaning" appeared in a prevalent location, and the Clorox logo was no longer part of the brand. However, the changes might have come too late as the brand was unable to regain customer interest. Their experience helps illustrate the importance of going beyond consumer relevance and understanding the potential for negative associations that consumers could make of a brand with social impact claims.

Saliency of Inconsistencies

As discussed earlier in the book, one of the most celebrated efforts to integrate a societal benefit into a brand belongs to Dove, the brand from Unilever. After almost 50 years of focusing on the development of their functional benefit as the cream bar that moisturizes the skin better than soap, the Campaign for Real Beauty challenged traditional standards of beauty in society which are often promoted by the marketing of beauty brands. Their first Super Bowl ad showed no product nor mention of their 50-year-old claim. This time, they used the 60 seconds to talk about self-esteem of young girls and the need to strengthen it. Their work elevated the issue to the national stage and instigated a debate made for social media. Their grassroots program acted on the need for change, providing training to thousands of educators able to influence young girls. In addition, their venture into a societal benefit was also strategic, as it came at a time when Unilever needed to build master brands under which they could promote more of their products. The campaign for real beauty was also a campaign to reposition Dove from a soap to a beauty brand. However, as their work became more popular, detractors and critics emerged, fuelled by the realization that the same company that was so elegantly standing for real beauty also owned Axe, a brand whose advertising messages often reinforced the same female stereotypes that Dove was fighting. Moreover, Greenpeace International, an external non-commercial stakeholder, spoofed the ad to show that Dove destroys the beauty of the rain forest in Indonesia and Malaysia with their extraction of palm oil, an important raw ingredient in the product, killing inhabitants such as chimpanzees. When competing on social impact, inconsistencies between the operations of a business and its brand claims will become more salient and should be quickly resolved—or, better, avoided in the first place. KFC faced a saliency of inconsistency challenge when it launched a program to raise funds for the Susan G. Komen Foundation and breast cancer research. Introduced with much publicity, the "Buckets for the Cure" initiative pledges to donate a percentage of proceeds from each pink bucket of fried chicken to the foundation. However, during the same period, the marketing team introduced a new menu item—the double-down sandwich—composed of two fried chicken breasts with bacon in the middle. Comments like this one began to circulate and spread online: *Come on, KFC, are you really saying you care about the wellbeing of women with this beast? Not true, retorts the Colonel. The target demo for the Double Down is men! So we should feel better knowing that the Double Down is a widow maker?*" In this case, the inconsistency between the nutritional value of the new product and their social impact initiative provoked enough criticism to threaten the program. In another example, Pepsi came under similar criticism after launching a promotion that donated $1.00 to the Juvenile Diabetes Research Foundation with the sale of every mega jug drink Pepsi, which carried more than 30 ounces of the sugar-rich product. Finally, the United States Labor Department took the State Street Corporation, the firm that commissioned a statue of a little girl on Wall Street called "fearless girl" as a symbol of women's empowerment, to court for payment discrimination against female employees.[4]

These examples help illustrate one of the unique aspects of competing on social impact. When competing on traditional claims like quality or price, marketers can succeed by focusing on commercial stakeholder needs be it consumers, retailers, or competitors. However, when integrating societal benefits and claims, they must consider the needs of non-commercial stakeholders, particularly those who care about the issue they are trying to support. Such stakeholders can become fans or foes, depending on how the brand embeds the societal benefit into its claims. It is unlikely that a societal benefit claim will persist in the market without generating some level of foes, but the goal of the brand manager is to maximize the fan-to-foe ratio. Many argue that for this to happen, the company needs to accumulate a set of "proof points" or evidence that the brand claims can be supported by investments and actions. While that is important, it is only a price of entry. In addition to the absence of evidence, the saliency of inconsistencies is sometimes harder to identify and manage. When a brand takes a stand on a social issue, it invites scrutiny by the market.

Critics will look not only for supporting evidence, but also for contrasting evidence. Inconsistencies between the firm's position and its actions in the past or by other brands in the portfolio will become salient and a source for foes. Sometimes, like in the case of Dove, those criticisms can be contained. But sometimes they can ruin the efforts regardless of their good intentions and support. Therefore, it is crucial for companies to ensure that their actions consistently reflect their social impact claims. Fortunately, spotting the risk of inconsistencies is something managers can do in advance of the program. For instance, the brand Bonafont, a water brand in Mexico, has been actively promoting women's empowerment and equality in the country. Like many other Latin American countries, Mexico has a history of general gender inequalities. The country ranks in the middle of the pack for gender equality among all nations in the world, but at the same time, it is ranked in the bottom 20 percent for economic participation and opportunity for women globally. Historically, Bonafont focused on women as their target audience and as a result, felt it had permission to play a role in resolving the gender gap. However, before the program was launched, Anna Rogova, the marketing director, conducted a thorough assessment of the internal employment practices toward women inside their company. She ensured that there were no inequities present in terms of pay, promotion, leadership representation, and talent development. In addition, she worked with the human resources team to revise the maternity leave policies, even casting guidelines for their advertising to be more inclusive of the diversity of women in the country. All those actions protected the brand against the saliency of inconsistencies and the potential criticisms it could generate. It also ensured they could stand more confidently behind their chosen social impact efforts in the market.

Politicization of the Offering

Dylan Mulvaney is a transgender influencer who became a social media personality, accumulating close to 11 million followers on TikTok by documenting her gender transition. In the Spring of 2023 Bud Light partnered with her in a TikTok video, and the response from conservative groups was swift, resulting in a national call for a boycott of what was the number one-selling beer brand in the country. It also led to a host of news headlines and negative social media buzz, including a video of musician Kid Rock shooting with a submachine gun at cases of the beer. Unknowingly, marketing managers placed their brand in the middle of a highly politicized issue, and over a short window of time, Bud Light beer sales were down 23 percent year-on-year, and Budweiser, another brand in the portfolio, declined by 8 percent. Shoppers switched to competitive brands, Coors and Miller, each growing by 17 percent, and Pabst which grew by 13 percent during the same period. Bud Light ended up losing 5 percentage points of market share by sales in the four weeks, while Budweiser lost 2 percentage points. As some branding experts such as Professors Jūra Liaukonytė and Brad Bronnenberg have noted, Bud Light's strategy appeared to be aimed at attracting younger customers to rejuvenate their older demographic. Yet Bud Light's customer base was not particularly conservative or liberal—it was situated somewhere in the middle and included a mix of both political ideologies. This diverse customer base meant that the brand needed to tread carefully when adopting any socially charged messaging. At the time, Bud Light had been losing market share as younger consumers increasingly migrated towards craft beer and seltzer drinks, which they perceived as more authentic, flavorful, and aligned with the values of the millennial and Gen Z demographics. Instead of directly addressing the core issue of changing younger consumers' preference, Bud Light assumed that featuring a transgender influencer in their marketing campaign would resonate with these younger customers. The logic behind this decision was likely rooted in the belief that younger generations are generally more progressive and supportive of LGBTQ+ rights. However, this approach proved to be misguided. Not only did the message fail to address the actual needs and preferences of younger customers, but it also enraged the older, more traditional segment of their customer base. This older demographic, who had been loyal to Bud Light for years, perceived the campaign as an unnecessary and provocative stance on a contentious social issue. Feeling alienated and betrayed, many of these long-standing customers abandoned the brand. The fallout from this misstep was severe. Bud Light not only failed to attract the younger consumers it was targeting, but it also lost a significant portion of its existing customer base. This dual blow resulted in a substantial loss of market share and eroded the brand's leading position in the beer industry.

In the increasingly polarized and politicized environment in which brands operate today, it is quite possible for a social impact effort to be mis-construed as an attack on a political view that can ignite a firestorm, most likely without intent. Earlier in the book, we discussed the example of the Coca-Cola Arctic Home program, which was the result of a partnership with the World Wildlife Foundation to protect polar bears in the Arctic. The program had a good brand-cause fit, owing to Coke's use of the ani-mal's image in their advertising since 1937. However, with it, Coke walked into the middle of a political debate on climate change. In the USA, a seg-ment of the population, particularly some on the right wing of the political spectrum, do not embrace the idea of climate change as a problem, let alone as a man-made problem. They saw in the Coke campaign not only support for the animals but also advocacy for a climate crisis. The topic ended up discussed both on the Senate floor and on radio programs. A number of retail customers refused to activate the campaign on the grounds that it promoted the idea of global warming. While managers were able to contain a larger-scale outcry from the right-wing media, they experienced first-hand the potential for politicization created when competing on social impact.

Traditional marketing efforts are largely uncontroversial. But when a brand takes a stand on a social issue that is heavily politicized, it can provoke strong reactions from individuals who hold opposing views. This can lead to polarization and backlash, with some stakeholders perceiving the brand as taking sides in a political debate. As Pepsi, Ben & Jerry's, Gillette, Starbucks, Nike, and many others have found, when social-impact initiatives strike the wrong chord, the response can damage the company's reputation and bottom line. In the realm of social media, where information spreads virally, these responses can quickly escalate into what are known as firestorms. A firestorm is a situation where a brand is suddenly inundated with intense and widespread criticism or backlash. A single post or public statement can trigger these firestorms which can gain momentum rapidly, sometimes within hours or even minutes. If such situations are ignored or mishandled, they can cause significant reputational damage to the brand, potentially eroding consumer trust and loyalty that took years to build.

Accusations of Greenwashing

The organizers of the Paris Olympics promised early on to make their Games the most eco-friendly in history. They committed to securing a second life for all the equipment and furniture used in venues, including 16,000 beds, 180,000 clothes hangers, 6,000 toilet roll holders, 1,400 microwaves, and 7,000 toilet brushes. The 30 boats that transported athletes along the Seine River during the Opening Ceremony were all electrically propelled. The medals were made from recycled gold and silver and procured by the Responsible Jewelry Council. According to Forbes magazine, Athletes in the Olympic Village experienced coffee tables made from recycled badminton shuttlecocks, bean bags made from parachute fabric, chairs made from recycled bottle caps and sofas made from Vauban barriers. Given these efforts, Olympic sponsors were motivated to follow suit. For instance, Toyota provided electric vehicles and transportation for athletes and officials during the games. Most efforts were celebrated. One was heavily criticized. Coca-Cola's attempt to contribute to the eco-friendly games resulted in broad accusations of what is frequently referred to as Greenwashing— falsified or misleading messages that deceive the public or hide other realities of a brand's social impact efforts. Their plan was to reduce single-use plastics by expanding the presence of fountain drink disposals and providing multi-used cups when fountains were not possible. The execution was reported[5] as "bizarre" and "surreal" by French environmental groups. Why? Because the solution was to serve beverages that were packaged in plastic bottles in what they named "eco-cups" which were also made from plastic. The plastic of the bottles was made from recycled material, and the plastic in the cups was durable and not intended for disposal. But most people just saw more plastic. The Coca-Cola team spent years planning the logistics for how to serve close to 20 million drinks to athletes and fans during the 16 days of the Games. Their project claims to have reduced plastic waste by half when compared to the 2012 London Olympics. Still, the accusations seem to have threatened the public view of their effort and resulted in one more example of the risk of social impact work. Greenwashing accusations are not just a reputational risk, they can also represent legal risks like in the case of H&M, which faced a class-action suit in New York based on claims that the fashion brand misrepresented the sustainability characteristics and benefits of their Conscious line of clothes.

The risk of greenwashing is well known, but many brands continue to experience it in part because brand managers have not internalized the differences between sustainability claims and more traditional product claims. When it comes to social impact benefits, it can be difficult to know the boundaries of what is viable to claim or balance intention with reality when seeking to attract customers. Also, stakeholders may react negatively if they suspect the firm's motives for adopting a societal benefit are not genuine. If stakeholders believe the brand is engaging in social actions merely as a promotional tactic or to capitalize on a trend, they may view the efforts as disingenuous, feeding into claims of greenwashing. This suspicion can undermine the brand's credibility and lead to negative perceptions. As Professor Cait Lamberton noted in her work on marketplace dignity, "It's erasing, in a sense, the contributions of people who had done incredibly brave things for instance, in the interest of civil rights — replacing their courageous actions with a trivial exchange."

Greenwashing claims can also arise when stakeholders perceive commercial interests as the primary driver of the brand's motives. Stakeholders understand that companies are profit-focused but feel that the brand behaves with manipulative intent if the company's initiative offers no apparent, tangible, or verifiable social benefit. Therefore, managers need to find a delicate balance between proving and claiming their social impact to customers.

Mitigating the Risks

During the planning of the Arctic Home program, the public affairs team at Coca-Cola did something unusual. They assumed that criticism was going to emerge as a result of their program and then tried to identify, as best they could, the source of the backlash by conducting a stakeholder analysis. Their work yielded an insight—that radio talk show hosts, particularly those that represented views from the right of the political spectrum, could initiate criticisms that might threaten the program. They concluded the risk was that a segment of stakeholders did not understand the intent and focus of the initiative, which was centered on protecting polar bears. Therefore, they started an effort to reach out to the most important radio talk show hosts and proactively explain the rationale and elements of the program. That action, while it did not eliminate criticism, helped contain it.

As illustrated by the experience of Coca-Cola managers, one way to mitigate the reputational risks of social impact is stakeholder mapping. The process identifies relevant stakeholders and evaluates their likely response, particularly whether they will accept and support the proposed social impact strategy. Unlike traditional marketing actions which typically target a specific audience segment, the scope of stakeholders who respond to brand social impact actions is much broader. These stakeholders include not only customers, but also employees, investors, partners, regulators, non-profit organizations and the public. Each of these groups may have different expectations and reactions to the brand's social impact initiatives. For instance, employees may feel a sense of pride and motivation if the brand's actions align with their personal values, while investors may be more concerned about the potential financial risks. This heterogeneity poses a significant challenge for brands as they must navigate the complex landscape of differing opinions and expectations. Consequently, brands face a risk of misalignment, especially when the social impact involves a divisive issue. Some of the brand's current and potential customers will inevitably disagree with the brand's societal benefit. If the brand speaks out loudly enough on a significant issue, it risks losing those customers[6]. This potential loss of customers is a critical consideration, as it can directly impact the brand's market share and profitability. Stakeholder maps, where managers assess the response by different commercial and non-commercial groups prior to the introduction of a social impact program, is a critical step in understanding the risk profile of the strategy and identifying mitigating actions. To perform a stakeholder mapping exercise, start by identifying the list of commercial and non-commercial stakeholders that could be impacted or interested in the social impact program. Commercial stakeholders are business partners, including retailers, distributors, employees, and customers. Non-commercial stakeholders are important constituents to the success of the program, but they are not linked to a brand, owing to its business activities. These include regulators, non-profit organizations, community or opinion leaders, and people working in the cause the brand seeks to support. After identifying the stakeholders, it is important to assess their potential influence and likely response to identify groups that might respond negatively to the brand's efforts. The last step is to identify a plan of action to engage the stakeholders at risk and involve them in the program in ways that might contribute to their support.

The proactive mapping and engagement of stakeholders is one approach, but it is not sufficient to mitigate all the potential risks. In fact, when competing on social impact, it is best to adopt the approach of Coke managers and assume your efforts will be criticized. The question is, can you identify that criticism and address it in time? Such action requires firms to build newer sense-and-response capabilities. Sense capabilities involve the ability to monitor and understand the reactions and sentiments of various stakeholders in real time. This includes leveraging advanced analytics and social listening tools to gauge public opinion and identify emerging issues before they escalate. Response capabilities, on the other hand, involve having the mechanisms and strategies in place to address these reactions effectively. This may include crisis communication plans, dedicated response teams, and clear protocols for engaging with stakeholders in a timely and transparent manner. For instance, in 2014, Coca-Cola aired an ad during the Super Bowl based on the song "America the Beautiful." However, in their version, the song was sung not only in English but also in Spanish, Tagalog, Mandarin, Hindi, Hebrew, Keres, French, and Arabic. It also showed images of different nationalities, races, and sexual orientations, including images of gay parents. It was an effort to support the LGBTQ+ community and diversity more broadly. Ben Deutsch, then Global Vice-President of Communications for the company, knew the ad was going to stir controversy. As a result, he and others set up a war room with social media managers who carefully monitored the conversations and consumer reactions. They were ready with scenarios and messages to respond quickly to different types of accusations and prevent the firestorm from spreading, which they did very successfully. Proactively preparing for the backlash and preparing response scenarios in advance can help managers navigate the turmoil that social impact programs can generate.

A third approach to mitigating the risk of backlash from social impact lies at the start of the process when selecting the societal need. As discussed earlier in the book, brand-cause fit and authenticity are necessary conditions for success when competing on social impact. Brands that act on societal issues without earned permission based on their heritage or product characteristics increase the risk of a firestorm. In Bud Light's case, the choice to feature a transgender influencer did not align with the traditional image and expectations of their existing customers. This created a disconnect that was both costly and damaging. Operating with a social impact "license" is crucial because it ensures that the brand's actions align with the expectations and values of its stakeholders. Gaining this permission involves several steps and considerations. First, brands need to establish trust with their stakeholders, ensuring that their actions do not violate expected norms. Respecting norms and avoiding incongruities in social impact choices is perhaps the lowest-cost method for gaining permission. When stakeholders trust a brand and see that it operates within acceptable boundaries, they are more likely to support its social initiatives. Brands can seek stakeholder permission for their societal benefits by engaging with their audience, using methods such as seeking stakeholder inputs or asking them to vote on important issues, thus gaining their involvement and buy-in. As brand permission tends to be social and normative, the likelihood of being perceived as violating norms decreases if peer stakeholders support the initiative. This social validation mitigates risks associated with controversial stances.

Brands build long-term capacity to gain permission by cultivating brand trust. Academic research suggests that trust is the antidote to stakeholder skepticism and reduces stakeholders' sensitivity to norm violations. For example, brands like Ben & Jerry's have carefully researched and vetted the social issues they support, earning permission to address even ideologically fraught topics such as anti-war and anti-white supremacy stances. This thorough approach helps them maintain credibility and support from their audience.

As discussed in our earlier chapters, brands also need to have a heritage and continually enrich it for a social impact strategy to be successful. Without a heritage in the societal issue, it is difficult for a brand to avoid skepticism. Of the many benefits a brand may confer, only a few are likely to have defined the brand from the start and be the core reason for its success. A careful evaluation of the brand's heritage can identify the most salient benefits the brand offers customers and isolate the social needs it is well-positioned to address. For instance, Patagonia has a long history of creating high-quality, durable products that require less frequent replacement, thereby conserving resources. This heritage has provided the foundation for Patagonia to become an activist in environmental issues. Over the years, the brand has not only supported environmental sustainability in its production processes but has also demarketed its products by placing ads during Black Friday in major media inviting people not to buy their products. It also provides grants to NGOs working on environmental issues through a self-imposed 1 percent "Earth tax for the planet." The consistency of these actions has helped build Patagonia's heritage as a champion of environmental causes.

Finally, brands need to identify the range and boundaries for their social purpose strategy. Establishing clear boundaries ensures that consumers see the brand's actions as credible and relevant. For example, Truist Bank can credibly address financial literacy issues, owing to its direct connection to financial services, but it would be hard-pressed to address climate change directly as its social impact strategy. Alternatively, consider a cigarette manufacturer like Altria opening a cigarette-branded research and treatment center specializing in throat or lung cancer. While the Truist example might be perceived as within its boundary, the Altria decision would test credulity and seem contradictory and disingenuous. To draw appropriate boundaries, brands must carefully evaluate which issues align with their core competencies and heritage. This alignment helps ensure that stakeholders perceive their social impact efforts as authentic and credible rather than opportunistic or hypocritical.

In conclusion, adopting a social impact strategy involves careful planning and consideration of stakeholder acceptance, brand heritage, and strategic boundaries. Importantly, these are all actions that are within the manager's control. While social impact can attract criticism and could be seen as risky by some leaders, the risks can be mitigated with careful planning and implementation. Brand managers can promote trust, ensure alignment between their actions and their brand heritage, and define the scope of their social impact efforts. By doing so, they can navigate the complex landscape of social impact initiatives and build stronger, more meaningful connections with their stakeholders. This strategic approach helps brands effectively contribute to societal well-being while maintaining credibility and support from their audience.

Notes

1 www.epa.gov/facts-and-figures-about-materials-waste-and-recycling.
2 Parker, Jeffrey R. et al. How product type and organic label structure combine to influence consumers' evaluations of organic foods. *Journal of Public Policy & Marketing, 40*(3) (2021), 419–428.
3 Luchs, Michael G. et al. The sustainability liability: Potential negative effects of ethicality on product preference. *Journal of Marketing, 74*(5) (2010), 18–31.
4 Gelles, D. (2017, October 6). 'Fearless Girl' statue's firm settles claims of under-paying women. *The New York Times.*
5 Lombard, L. (2024, August 7). Greenwash games? French public points finger at Coca-Cola over Olympics plastic waste. *The Guardian.*
6 Hydock, C., Paharia, N., & Blair, S. (2020). Should your brand pick a side? How market share determines the impact of corporate political advocacy. *Journal of Marketing Research, 57*(6): 1135–1151.

Chapter 11

Brands Practicing Social Activism

Sparked by incidents such as the tragic killing of George Floyd, corporate social responsibility in general and social impact in particular have recently undergone a significant transformation. Some customers now expect firms to play a more proactive role in society than ever before (Edelman, 2020[1]; Vox, 2020[2]). This expectation marks a departure from the traditional view of businesses as entities primarily focused on profit. Today, there are consumer groups that look to companies to contribute positively to social issues, reflecting their values and taking tangible actions toward societal improvement.

Reflecting this shift, a 2021 survey among American consumers found that a vast majority—75 percent—prefer firms that take a stand on social issues (YouGov, 2021). This preference indicates a growing trend where consumers are not only mindful of the products and services they purchase but also increasingly interested in the ethical and social stances of the companies they support. In this new landscape, a company's willingness to engage in social advocacy is redefining brand loyalty.

In response some companies are evolving into activists themselves, addressing social problems in their own unique ways (Sarkar and Kotler, 2018[3]). This evolution can be seen in various forms, from corporate donations to social causes and advocacy campaigns to integrating social responsibility into their core business strategies. Firms have launched initiatives that tackle issues such as racial equality, environmental sustainability, gender equity, and more, aiming to make a meaningful impact on society.

However, taking a proactive stance on social issues and incorporating activism into marketing strategies is fraught with challenges and potential pitfalls. Activist actions can polarize opinions, leading to strong negative reactions from those who disagree with the stance taken. This can result in a loss of customers, negative publicity, and even boycotts. Additionally, there is the risk of being perceived as insincere or opportunistic, particularly if the activism appears to be more of a marketing ploy than a genuine effort to drive change. Customers may question the true intentions behind the activism, leading to skepticism and distrust.

DOI: 10.4324/9781003383246-12

Therefore, brands are caught in a dilemma between the rising demands for brand activism and the inherent risks involved. As we discussed in the previous chapter, engaging in activism can attract significant scrutiny and backlash from segments of the population that may not share the same views. This can lead to potential boycotts, negative publicity, and a divisive impact on the customer base. This delicate balance leaves many companies uncertain about how to incorporate activism effectively and beneficially into their marketing strategies. They must consider how to align their activism with their brand identity and values without alienating key stakeholders. The challenge lies in being genuine and consistent in their messaging and ensuring that consumers perceive their activist efforts as authentic rather than opportunistic.

For some companies, activism is a natural extension of their mission and values, seamlessly integrated into their brand narrative. For others, it might be a strategic decision driven by market demands and the changing expectations of their customer base. In either case, brands must carefully manage the commitment to social responsibility and activism to avoid pitfalls and maximize positive outcomes.

It is important to note, activism is not appropriate for all brands, nor is it a requirement for good growth. Leaders that decide to engage in it will need to develop a comprehensive approach that includes understanding the audience, communicating clearly, and committing long-term to the causes they support. Moreover, firms must also consider the alignment between the activist actions with their core mission and values. When consumers perceive actions as inconsistent with or contradictory to the brand's established identity, it can create confusion and dilute the brand message. Ensuring that activism is not just a superficial add-on, but an integrated part of the company's values and operations, is crucial for maintaining authenticity and credibility.

By doing so, they can build stronger connections with their customers, foster loyalty, and contribute positively to societal change. As the landscape of corporate social responsibility continues to evolve, the ability to effectively balance activism with business objectives will become increasingly crucial for brands aiming to thrive in this new era of consumer expectations.

Historically, the prevailing belief has been that companies should avoid engaging in socio-political debates to maintain a neutral stance that appeals to a broader customer base. This conventional wisdom has guided many firms in their communication strategies emphasizing a focus on their products, services, and core business values rather than controversial social issues. The rationale behind this approach is to minimize the risk of alienating any segment of their customer base, thereby ensuring market stability and broad appeal.

The literature on corporate activism paints a more dire picture, acknowledging that a firm's activism inherently involves significant risk (e.g. Bhagwat et al., 2020[4]; Hydock et al., 2020[5]; Mukherjee and Althuizen, 2020[6]; Vredenburg et al., 2020[7]). Engaging in activism can expose a company to a variety of potential repercussions. For instance, taking a stand on a divisive issue can alienate existing customers whose values do not align with the firm's position (Hydock et al., 2020; Mukherjee and Althuizen, 2020). These customers may feel betrayed or marginalized, leading to a decline in loyalty and a potential loss of business.

Furthermore, activism can raise suspicion among customers regarding the true intentions behind the firm's actions (Vredenburg et al., 2020). Consumers are increasingly savvy and may question whether a company's activism is genuinely motivated by a commitment to social change or if it is merely a strategic ploy to capitalize on current trends. This skepticism can undermine the trust and authenticity that brands strive to build, leading to reputational damage.

Another significant risk associated with corporate activism is the potential to signal a deviation from the firm's core mission and values (Bhagwat et al., 2020). When a company's activist actions appear inconsistent with its established identity, it can create confusion and dilute the brand's message. This inconsistency can be particularly damaging if stakeholders perceive the activism as incongruent with the company's primary business objectives.

Overall, the consensus in the literature is that a firm's activism is likely to provoke strong negative reactions from opposing customers and relatively moderate positive responses from supporters, which could result in a negativity bias (Hydock et al., 2020). This negativity bias implies that the adverse reactions from those who disagree with the firm's stance may outweigh the favorable responses from those who support it. The implications of this are significant, as the net effect of activism could potentially harm the brand more than it benefits it.

Yet, not taking action can also pose challenges. Consumers and employees can perceive silence on social issues as a lack of empathy or a refusal to acknowledge the realities that many customers face. This perception can erode trust and loyalty, as some of today's consumers are increasingly looking for brands to not only provide products or services, but also reflect their values and support causes they believe in. Companies that choose not to engage with social issues risk appearing out of touch or indifferent, which can have long-term negative effects on their brand image and customer relationships.

In light of these complexities, companies are left pondering a critical question: If they cannot afford to stay silent on social issues yet find the direct path to activism fraught with risk, what should their approach be? How can they navigate this complex landscape in a way that resonates positively with their audience while minimizing potential downsides? Finding a balanced strategy that addresses societal concerns and aligns with the brand's values and objectives is crucial in today's socially conscious marketplace. This might involve a more nuanced approach to activism, where firms engage in meaningful dialogue with stakeholders, commit to long-term social initiatives, and transparently communicate their efforts and progress. By doing so, companies can build stronger, more resilient relationships with their customers and contribute to positive social change without compromising their brand integrity.

Our research (Kim & Bharadwaj, 2022[8]) coding 1,407 brands' activist posts on Instagram from October 2010 to February 2022 using Bidirectional Encoder Representation from Transformers models and causal inference techniques provides a grounded understanding of how brands can improve customer responses toward brand activism. We believe that a brand can significantly enhance customer responses toward its activist initiatives by ensuring that its actions adhere to four critical principles:

Comprehensibility: For brand activism to be effective, it must be easily understandable to the target audience. This means that the messaging should be clear, concise, and devoid of ambiguity. When customers can easily grasp the purpose and intent behind the brand's activism, they are more likely to engage positively. The use of straightforward language, relatable narratives, and transparent communication strategies plays a vital role in making the activism comprehensible.

Factual Support: Actions supported by factual information tend to garner greater credibility and trust from customers. In an era where misinformation can spread rapidly, grounding activist statements and campaigns in verifiable data and evidence is crucial. Providing statistics, expert testimonials, and credible sources can bolster the authenticity of the brand's activism, making it more persuasive and trustworthy in the eyes of the public.

Congruent Tangible Actions: It is not enough for brands to merely voice their support for social causes; they must also take tangible actions that are congruent with their stated positions. This involves implementing initiatives, policies, or programs that demonstrate a genuine commitment to the cause. For instance, a brand advocating for environmental sustainability should adopt eco-friendly practices in its operations. Such congruent actions reinforce the brand's message and show that the activism is not just performative but part of a sincere effort to effect change.

Legitimacy Based on Previous Activist Trajectory: The legitimacy of a brand's activism is significantly influenced by its historical actions and consistency in supporting social causes. Consumers are more likely to perceive brands that have a well-documented history of engaging in activist efforts as genuine and committed. This historical legitimacy helps build a strong foundation of trust and reliability. For example, a brand with a longstanding commitment to diversity and inclusion is better positioned to be credible when it launches a new initiative in this area. Customers are more likely to respond positively when they see a continuous and authentic trajectory of activism.

In conclusion, this study underscores the importance of clarity, factual support, congruent actions, and historical legitimacy in enhancing customer responses to brand activism. By incorporating these elements into their strategies, brands can navigate the complex landscape of social activism more effectively, building stronger connections with their customers and fostering positive social change.

Notes

1 Edelman Trust Barometer Special Report: Brand Trust in 2020. Edelman website. Published June 25, 2020. Accessed December 20, 2024.
2 Blackout Tuesday 2020: One year later, what have companies done since? Vox website. Published June 2, 2021.
3 Sarkar, C. & Kotler, P. *Brand Activism: From Purpose to Action*. IDEA BITE PRESS, 2018.
4 Bhagwat, Y., Warren, N. L., Beck, J. T., & Watson, G. F., IV. Corporate Sociopolitical Activism and Firm Value. *Journal of Marketing*, 2020, *84*(5), 1–21.
5 Hydock, C., Paharia, N., & Blair, S. Should Your Brand Pick a Side? How Market Share Determines the Impact of Corporate Political Advocacy. *Journal of Marketing Research*, 2020, *57*(6), 1135–1151.
6 Mukherjee, S. & Althuizen, N. Brand Activism: Does Courting Controversy Help or Hurt a Brand?. *International Journal of Research in Marketing*, 2020, *37*(4), 772–788.
7 Vredenburg, J., Kapitan, S., Spry, A., & Kemper, J. A. Brands Taking a Stand: Authentic Brand Activism or Woke Washing?. *Journal of Public Policy & Marketing*, 2020, *39*(4), 444–460.
8 Brand Activism and Consumer Responses.

Chapter 12

Leadership Practices

George-Axelle Broussillon Matschinga's journey into diversity, equity, and inclusion (DEI) began over 20 years ago. Starting her career at L'Oréal, she was instrumental in developing and implementing the company's first global diversity policies across Europe and the U.S. In February 2020 she took on the role of Vice President of Diversity, Equity, and Inclusion at Sephora, contributing to the formation of one of the most inclusive brands in business. Under her leadership, Sephora crafted and launched its inaugural holistic DEI strategy and governance framework. A significant milestone came in January 2021 with the public release of a Sephora-led industry study on racial bias in retail. Among the many findings, the report revealed that three in five BIPOC (Black, Indigenous, and People of Color) customers felt unwelcome in retail settings, many times deciding not to return. Armed with these insights, George-Axelle and other Sephora leaders set an ambitious objective: to transform the shopping experience for BIPOC customers and enhance inclusivity throughout its operations. The team put into motion nothing short of a transformation. They introduced training programs focused on DEI, implicit bias, and cultural sensitivity to equip employees with the necessary skills to foster an inclusive in-store environment. They also increased the hiring of BIPOC store managers and staff to ensure that their workforce reflected the diversity of its customer base. Then came the signing of the 15 Percent Pledge—a movement founded by Aurora James in 2020 that challenged retailers to allocate at least 15 percent of their inventory to Black-owned brands. Since then, Sephora has more than doubled its Black-owned brand offerings. This initiative led to an expanded range of skincare and cosmetic products catering to all skin tones. It also helped enhance the Accelerate program, which helps BIPOC-owned startups enter and scale brands in the market. The team also established guidelines for marketing that included new diversity standards for talent casting, social media content, production, branding elements, and partner selection, ensuring that its engagement efforts were relevant to its diverse clientele.

Their commitment to inclusion was not limited to the company. They also aspired to change the industry. Under George-Axelle's guidance,

DOI: 10.4324/9781003383246-13

Sephora shared its research at industry forums, culminating in the 2022 launch of the Mitigate Racial Bias in Retail Charter in collaboration with the nonprofit organization Open to All. This charter, now endorsed by more than 80 major retailers, promotes and fosters inclusive experiences for shoppers of color. Collectively, these actions have positioned marketplace inclusion as a strategic imperative for Sephora, contributing to a twofold increase in revenues since the initiative's inception.

In 2023 we conducted an assessment to measure Sephora's inclusion maturity across 72 business practices spanning five dimensions: organization, marketing strategy and planning, commercial practices, brand communication practices, and advocacy and support for communities of color. The results were outstanding, indicating that inclusivity had become deeply integrated into Sephora's operations—from talent acquisition and product offerings to customer experience design and performance metrics. The remarkable progress made by the team at Sephora to foster inclusion in its operations and its industry required more than a commitment. It required leaders like George-Axelle and others inside the company to collaborate well with non-profit partners, balance long and short-term thinking, build cross-sectional coalitions, behave authentically in the market, and, at times, hold the tension between business and societal value. In fact, our own research finds those actions as defining characteristics of leaders that have been effective in helping their companies find good growth. Aspiring social impact leaders would benefit from reflecting on how they can embody these principles in their own practices.

Principle 1: Understanding the Non-Profit Mindset.

In 1992 Peter Sealy and Sergio Zyman led a transformation in advertising at The Coca-Cola Company. For the first time, a major brand moved away from the advertising agency system and hired the Creative Artists Agency (CAA), a talent agency, to create its global campaign. Out of that effort came one of the most iconic campaigns in Coca-Cola's history—"Always Coca-Cola." The company assembled a pool of recognized film directors and creative talent to develop the work. Most of the messages were used across countries, but only one stood the test of time, and versions of it are still used today, more than thirty years later—the polar bear ad. The messages have changed, but the animated polar bear commercials became a staple of the brand and its holiday campaigns during the wintertime. They were one of the most differentiated assets the brand had created and loved by many, except the scientists working for the World Wildlife Fund. For the WWF, educating the public on the realities and risks faced by polar bears as a result of climate change and the melting of ice caps was of preeminent importance. Therefore, they saw the Coca-Cola ads contributing to a false narrative. For instance, some of the ads portrayed polar bears and penguins together, even though the two species live on opposite continents. The differences between the marketing team at Coke and the scientist team at WWF became important when the Coca-Cola CEO, Muhtar Kent, announced the partnership we discussed earlier in the book designed to raise funds to build a refuge in the Arctic. At that time, Coca-Cola and WWF clashed in their vision for what needed to be communicated. Coca-Cola managers wanted to entertain. WWF managers wanted to educate. Key to the resolution of the conflict was one of the persons responsible for managing the relationship between the two organizations, Abigail Rodgers. While she had worked for many years as a marketing director at Coca-Cola, her career started as a history teacher. Because profit maximization was not the main goal in the field of education, she developed an understanding and appreciation for social impact, not just business impact. She was instrumental in helping the Coca-Cola and WWF teams find a way to resolve the conflict of mission. The solution was to partner with the award-winning documentary filmmaker MacGillivray Freeman and produce a moving real story about the life of polar bears. It carried the emotion of the Coca-Cola messages but the realism and education that WWF needed. This solution was, in part, possible because Abigail Rodgers and her team at Coke were able to understand the non-profit mindset when managing the partnership.

Coca-Cola leaders are masterful at partnering, a capability its CEO once described as one of its most critical avenues to success. They partner with retailers, food service companies, technology firms, and thousands of event organizers, including some at a global scale, such as the International Olympic Committee and FIFA. But most of those partnerships share a key ingredient—commercial incentives. At the end of the day, everyone involved is looking to sell more or grow more. Partnering with non-profit organizations is also essential in social impact work, but they rarely prioritize commercial motives. Instead, they are mission-oriented and focused on factors that would advance their cause, not their profits. When working for a brand, effective social impact leaders need to understand the non-profit mindset and their incentives in order to craft partnership structures that work. For instance, how will the partnership impact the perception of the donor community, not just the consumer community? In the case of the WWF and Coca-Cola partnership, they conducted a survey among different types of donors to understand how their partnership may impact their affiliation with WWF. The findings reinforce the WWF stance that a program designed to educate would have a significantly more positive impact on donors than a program designed to entertain. Many of the marketing or brand leaders we interviewed as part of our research had previously worked at non-profit organizations. They understood well the differences in goals, motivations, and missions between their internal business stakeholders and non-profit partners.

Principle 2: Think Long Term, Act Short Term

Many growth managers operate in the constant pursuit of short-term goals, be it quarterly sales quotas or revenue targets. In contrast, social impact benefits are often associated with actions that create positive results in the future. This time difference generates a barrier to the adoption of social impact strategies because managers responsible for the business results do not see the construction of societal benefits as central to their success. Effective social impact leaders resolve this tension by thinking long term but acting short term. This means they recognize the long-term implications and potential benefits of enacting societal benefits, but they require their team actions to have an impact in the now. Take, for instance, the work by the marketing team for the SmartWater and Dasani brands in the United States. The bottled water industry offers many benefits, including access to clean drinking water or convenience for consumers in places lacking access to clean water. However, they also represent a major source of environmental problems. Plastic bottles rank as the third most collected plastic waste item in the Ocean Conservancy's list of pollution causes impacting the sea and sea life. According to a report by the Organization for Economic Co-operation and Development, 72 percent of plastic produced ends up in landfills, and most require hundreds of years to decompose, creating a lasting impact on the environment. The team was responsible for driving sales growth and increased consumption among consumers. They were aware that environmental concerns posed a threat to the sustainability of their business. Keeping the long-term in mind, they acted with a short-term mindset, working with their R&D team to develop new packaging solutions that could reduce the problem. While it was not economically feasible to remove plastic altogether, they explored the option of removing the use of virgin material by developing a bottle made from 100 percent recycled plastic. We helped them conduct concept tests with consumers and found that 32 percent of consumers in urban U.S. markets were already making purchase decisions by prioritizing reduced plastic in water bottles. Importantly, some segments of consumers reported a 4x increase in purchase intent when presented with a recycled plastic bottle option vs. the traditional plastic bottle. Armed with those statistics, they worked with bottlers in Texas to launch a pilot of the bottle made from recycled plastic. The results were remarkable. The brand experienced a 20 percent increase in sales, leading the team to expand the use of the bottle across the country. Today, bottles made of recycled plastic are quickly becoming the new standard, and while not yet representing a complete solution to the plastic pollution problem, they are reducing the generation of new plastic. The success of this team in turning social impact into business impact was partly driven by their ability to see the long term but act in the short term. Social impact leaders who help others realize how societal benefits can generate results in the now are more effective in mobilizing their organizations toward action and securing the necessary resources to do so. Appeals to broader social or moral responsibilities have a role to play, but rarely do they result in sustained support. While frequently presented as a tradeoff, the balance of long-term thinking and short-term action can help leaders unlock the potential of social impact.

Principle 3: Building Cross-Sectional Coalitions

In a city surrounded by successful professional sports teams like the Phillies, the Eagles, and the 76ers, the Philadelphia Souls had difficulty finding their fan base as an arena football team during the early 2000s. One of the owners, the singer Jon Bon Jovi, wanted to differentiate the team by actively investing in the community. He convinced the other owners to focus their efforts on fighting the homelessness crisis impacting the city. However, instead of simply donating money to a local organization, he reached out to local leaders to find someone who knew the homeless issue well enough to guide them on how to contribute in a relevant way. While exploring the subject, they came across Sister Mary Scullion, co-founder and executive director of Project H.O.M.E. Sister Scullion had been working for decades to serve the homeless in Philadelphia and understood well the gaps in the system set up to help them. She became a partner to the team owners and Jon Bon Jovi as they designed their programs and eventually launched the JBJ Soul Kitchen. The restaurant has no prices on the menu. People decide how much to pay, and in doing so, they make sure that their food was always available to serve homeless people or those with limited resources. By relying on the experience and guidance of Sister Mary Scullion, the partners of the Philadelphia Souls demonstrated an important practice of social impact leaders—the pursuit of cross-sectional coalitions. Partnerships are a common way of growing a business, but as discussed earlier in this chapter, they tend to occur among people or organizations that have a shared interest in commercial gains. A cross-sectional coalition is different because it is composed of people from different sectors, including regulators, non-profits, or community leaders working together to design or implement a social impact program. We saw this practice present across many of the successful programs we studied, including the effort by Kathleen Dunlop to create a cross-sectional coalition with doctors working in the refugee camps to guide the design of the Vaseline Healing Project. This partnership approach is essential in helping managers identify the best ways of contributing to a cause.

Principle 4: Nourish authenticity, not just publicity.

When Procter and Gamble introduced its campaign to sponsor the Olympic games for the first time in 2012, no one accused them of not being committed or authentic about their investment. It did not seem like consumers expected P&G managers to be former Olympic athletes or required the company to have a long history of support for the games in order to become a global sponsor. Similarly, no one seems to criticize State Farm managers for sponsoring the NBA despite the fact that there are no former NBA players in the brand management team or a history of sports associations within the company. However, that expectation is different when a brand associates itself with a social cause. Consumers and critics are quick to assess the level of authenticity and judge the intentions of the brand or company when seeking to do good, not just sell goods. Social impact leaders need to anticipate that expectation and proactively nurture and protect the authenticity of their efforts. Publicity without authenticity is likely to lead to backlash and accusations of commercial intent, diluting the effect of social impact efforts and, at times, creating a Public Relations nightmare for managers.

Alex Thompson, head of Public and Community Relations at the retailer REI, had an intuitive sense of the importance of authenticity in the work they did with environmental causes. He and his team used a simple four-question framework to ensure their social impact actions were authentic to their brand and company. First, does REI have permission to participate in a particular societal area of interest? That permission could come from their community, their heritage, or their expertise. But without it, he felt their ambitions would fall flat. As discussed earlier, managers normally do not worry about permission from fans before sponsoring a sporting or cultural event. Yet, getting involved in societal causes is different and requires a level of credibility that can only be earned, not purchased.

The second question Alex used concerned timing. Is the cultural context the right one for the brand to become involved with and discuss a particular issue? For instance, are many people already talking about the issue in ways that would invalidate the brand's contribution? Or will the brand be the first and therefore, need to be more attentive to potential risks that have yet to be revealed?

The third question is—does the brand have the power to make a difference? Can the brand bring anything different or new to the societal issue in a way that can make a real contribution? Lastly, do we have a responsibility to act? That speaks to the connection between the societal impact and the business. Is the brand a part of the issue? For instance, bottled water brands contribute to plastic pollution. In the case of Dove, leaders found that skincare brands and their advertising often contributed to misperceptions of beauty.

In the case of REI, the team believed that retail stores and their promotion during the Thanksgiving holiday season contributed significantly to a culture of consumerism. In fact, the Black Friday event is a retail store event. Therefore, they believed they had a direct role to play in addressing it. "*We absolutely have permission as a Co-op because we're independent. We think that in the long term, we're not accountable to shareholders. And our mission is to get people outdoors,*" reflected Alex. He also spoke to us about the fact that, culturally, there was an opportunity because of a growing discontent with consumerism. Finally, they felt that as an out-door retailer, they had an enormous amount of leverage to influence the issue and even a responsibility to do so. The four-question framework helped inform their decision to design and launch the "Opt Outside" program we discussed in Chapter 8—a plan to close their stores nation-wide the day after Thanksgiving and encourage people to go outside instead of shopping. The program was a smashing success, going viral on social media and inspiring numerous retailers to follow suit. By letting the questions in their framework guide their social impact program, they ensured that their actions were perceived as authentic by key stake-holders, including employees, members, and consumers at large.

Principle 5: Hold the Tension

Leading social impact work inside a for-profit environment can be difficult, particularly in environments where creating societal benefits is perceived as a distraction from building the business. We noticed an interesting pattern in many of our conversations with managers and students on the subject of social impact in business—a certain discomfort when linking the topic of societal benefits with business benefits. When asked about the reason for changing a product offering or introducing a new service, managers were quick to discuss the business opportunity they were trying to capture. Maybe it was to target a new customer segment or stop the erosion of customers leaving for a competitor. Yet when asked about social impact investments, managers tended to rely on a different type of answer—"because it is the right thing to do," as if the topic was exempt from accountability by being societal in nature, or at risk of losing authenticity because it was profitable. That division of purpose between social impact and business impact initiatives, with one being considered profit-driving and the other as simply the right thing to do, is a limiting behavior for people seeking to lead social impact inside a firm. Delivering on the sales objectives, protecting the profitability of your business, or winning in the market with better products is also the right thing to do. Many effective leaders of social impact we studied, including Alex Thompson, Kathleen Dunlop, and Anna Rogova, understood that intuitively and were able to hold the tension between social value and business value. They had no problem presenting the business case for a social impact investment to a room filled with finance managers and then discussing the moral case and social responsibility that justified their involvement to a room full of employees or non-profit partners. Effective social impact leaders hold the tension between delivering on commercial goals and contributing to socie-tal needs. They are unapologetic on both the business and moral cases to create societal benefits with their investments and see it as simply a new way of growing a business.

The principles of understanding the non-profit mindset, pursuing short-term results, building cross-sectional coalitions, nurturing authenticity, and holding the tension can help aspiring leaders of social impact in business influence their organizations effectively and thrive in the pursuit of good growth.

Chapter 13

Finding "Good Growth"—the SunTrust Case

The impact of the Great Recession of 2008 reverberated throughout the entire financial services world. According to the Washington Post, Americans lost an estimated $9.8 trillion in retirement savings, while the market overall lost nearly $7.8 trillion. When Bill Rogers took over as CEO of SunTrust in 2011, both the banking industry and SunTrust were still on the path of financial recovery, and consumer trust in banks was at an all-time low. In 2011, according to an industry report 36 percent of Americans had little or no confidence in the U.S. banking system, and 33 percent of customers felt their banks weren't helpful at all.

Shortly after Bill Rogers began his tenure as CEO, he had an experience that made the lack of consumer trust in financial institutions very real for him. "*I was in one of our branches spending half a day with our teammates,*" he recalled. "*The branch manager worked with us for a long time, and as the day was ending and we were talking, she took her badge off. I said, 'What are you doing?' And she said, 'Well, I have to stop at the grocery store, I have to stop to pick up my child, and I don't want people to know that I work for a bank.' I was shocked. She gave me an honest answer, which is right, but that's not the kind of company that we want to work for nor the industry that we want to be in. She was embarrassed, not only of working for SunTrust, but of being part of the financial services industry.*"

This encounter left a strong impression on Bill, and he frequently returned to that story when he explained why SunTrust needed to think about the next phase of growth in different terms. They needed a purpose that could reconnect them to the positive impact they can have in society. He sent the branch manager a note that same day, along with his commitment to helping SunTrust teammates recover their pride for an organization that was core to the fabric of many communities. He selected three senior executives to help lead the effort, one from Marketing, one from Human Resources, and one from Geographic Banking.

The initial goal was to find common language for how leaders thought about the company, along with the larger purpose that defined their organization. The team led numerous conversations through town halls and interviews and conducting a great deal of research to

DOI: 10.4324/9781003383246-14

understand how other companies were approaching similar efforts. At times it felt like a slow and iterative process ran counter to the way that Bill Rogers was used to working. "I'm very structured, and I like timelines, deadlines, and specific objectives," he recalled. "However, as we got into this work, it didn't lend itself to that type of management approach. A lot of the progress made was really organic, which frankly was uncomfortable for me." Instead of a linear plan with progress reports, what the team managed seemed like an ongoing cycle of divergent and convergent efforts with continuous alterations. They would read the material, interview team members, and hold whiteboard sessions to share initial drafts and solicit reactions to concepts and terms. There was a lot of back and forth on ideas, with people challenging each other as they added principles and values to the list. Those exchanges were essential for adding precision to the language and clarity to the action plan.

The results from the feedback pointed the team to the idea of examining and defining the bank's purpose beyond a sole focus on the bottom line and consider its potential social, not just economic, impact. They coalesced around a set of statements to represent their beliefs about the company. Ideas emerged that centered on client needs, the importance of teamwork and cooperation, and the attention needed for execution excellence. As leaders aligned on a set of principles and values, the need for a general statement that could serve as an umbrella became apparent. The team wanted a statement to clarify the bank's reason to exist in the first place.

One early option was to focus on helping people with their financial literacy, which was a common problem among banking institutions. However, the need for financial literacy did not address the underlying lack of trust nor the root causes impacting the community. Also, Bill worried that describing people as financially illiterate would shift the blame to them rather than fault the dire conditions many were forced to experience. Instead, he thought it was critical to understand the current status of the world as well as the most pressing needs emerging from the crisis. "The amount of people who don't have $2,000 saved for an emergency represented a third to nearly half of Americans," Bill remarked. "A similar percentage reported not having any money saved for retirement. The number of people living paycheck to paycheck was high. There is a societal issue here, and SunTrust was uniquely positioned to play a more pivotal role." Bill felt strongly that the societal needs to focus on were issues of financial stress, security, and confidence, not just literacy. A social impact strategy began to emerge, which they referred to as their purpose.

To help communicate its social impact work and values, SunTrust hired the consulting company Brighthouse. One of the outputs of their work came to be known as the "purpose flag." The graphic was placed in offices and conference rooms and provided an overview as well as a constant reminder of the bank's principles, values, and behaviors, all under the statement of

Lighting the Way to Financial Wellbeing. That phrase became the articulation of SunTrust's promise to shareholders and came to represent an ambition that the teammates could rally around.

Embedding Purpose Inside the Firm

> "I can't underscore it enough that the company purpose has to be core to your business. Then, you have to recruit people who have that same sort of passion. You have to align incentives around it. You have to align your practices around it."
>
> Bill Rogers

Identifying and describing the firm's purpose was the first step. Making it become the way the bank grew its business was another challenge altogether. To become a purpose-driven company that balances business and social impact, it was not enough to have a statement that people could remember. The bank needed to embed the intention behind the statement into the fabric of the firm, its behavior, and its many management decisions. This next phase was not easy, partly because the team faced resistance from external analysts and, more importantly, its own leaders and board members. Bill recalled that some thought of the effort as simply a marketing campaign or as a phase that would pass: "I would hear people say, let's just all buckle down, and we'll get through it; it's something Bill and his crazy team want to do, it's a slogan, it's a logo and we'll get through that." This tension existed in part because the bank was facing pressures on performance, and the connection between social impact work and day-to-day work was initially unclear. In many ways, it felt more philanthropic than strategic. Board members were similarly skeptical at the beginning. As a result, Bill did not make the focus on social impact a central part of the bank's strategy during his first year. Cost reduction, operating excellence, customer retention, and other business strategies took precedence in regular calls and meetings. However, Bill slowly started to include updates about the integration of social impact into company practices in conversations with the board. He waited even longer to bring the discussion to investors and analysts. Part of this decision was informed by a "Be-Do-Say" framework, which suggested that before the team communicated its social impact work externally, it needed to make sure the work was real and practiced within its own organization. This approach helped ensure they protected the credibility of the work as it scaled across more areas of the bank.

About a year into the effort and after many interactions with clients, Bill saw teammates begin to embrace the social impact purpose as part of their everyday roles. This evolution gave him the confidence to make the work more central in his discussions with all key audiences, internal and external. He also began to consider structural changes that could turn the social impact strategy into action. For instance, the leadership team had created a department responsible for integration but placed it inside the SunTrust Foundation which contributed to the perception that purpose work was an extension of philanthropy. Yet, for SunTrust, social impact purpose was a way for how to think about the business they were in and how they would pursue growth. As a result, they decided to separate the social impact work from the CSR and philanthropic efforts of the bank and focus the new role solely on the integration of purpose into the firm.

Over time, four unique channels of integration emerged, each with a separate leader accountable. First was the Teammate Channel, which worked closely with the human resources team to embed the purpose strategy into the culture, benefits, incentives, and practices of the organization. Second, the Consumer Channel group was responsible for partnering with the product marketing team to determine ways of integrating the social impact strategy into the products and services of the bank. This group helped marketers consider changes to more closely align their work with the purpose of the firm. The leader of this effort explained it in this way: "If we are really standing for lighting the way to financial wellbeing, when people get declined for a loan why do we just say 'sorry you didn't get the loan' instead of saying, 'sorry you did not currently qualify but we hope to be able to partner with you in the future. As a result, we offer our free financial education course, which can help improve your credit score.' Even if they don't become our clients, they will still be better off as individuals. So that's the lens the Consumer Channel team was trying to help the product team use."

A third was the Wholesale Channel, which focused on extending the employee financial well-being programs to other corporate clients and companies. Lastly, there was the Community Channel which worked closely with the foundation and the community volunteer teams managing not-for-profit partners. As an example of how this team worked, many owners of micro-businesses or self-employed individuals lacked the tools or means to achieve greater financial well-being. Yet many were also distrustful of large financial institutions and the team could not use their traditional methods to reach them. As a result, the Community Channel team established a partnership with the Operation Hope organization to assign in-branch counselors in key locations. The team became a critical conduit in scaling the bank's social impact initiatives with this hard-to-reach population.

Another aspect of the implementation strategy that Bill promoted was the connection of the social impact purpose initiatives to the job of individual managers. The risk was that most people would consider it a social responsibility or philanthropic activity as opposed to a part of their job or an element of the bank's growth and operations. To make the financial stress problem more real, the team decided to conduct an internal assessment of the financial well-being of SunTrust teammates. Bill was doubtful at the beginning, thinking that the issues of financial stress and insecurity would be more salient in the community than among his own workforce. He explained, "I wanted to start with the community because I assumed that as a financial institution, the issue would not impact us in the same way. However, I was proven wrong." The level of financial confidence among SunTrust teammates was only 40 percent, which was roughly the same as the general population. Bill remarked: "It was scary to think that six out of ten people in our team advising clients were, in fact, experiencing their own financial instability." This finding provided a tangible reason for many in the bank to buy into the social impact work and commit to the implementation of programs across the business.

Bill wanted the team to move quickly from insight into action, so he spearheaded a plan to close the financial security gap among teammates. They found an external partner called Eight Pillars, which focused on providing financial planning education. After running the program with Sun-Trust teammates, Bill decided to acquire the company and hire its CEO to lead the financial wellness programs at the bank.

The formation of an internal financial fitness program for teammates was an important enabler of integration during the first years of the social impact work. The program boosted the financial wellness of teammates and provided data to assess progress. It made the social impact work tangible and relevant for many, and enabled the leadership team to demonstrate its commitment in a tangible way. For instance, teammates who completed the program would receive $1,000 to help them establish an emergency savings account—a strong message of commitment and support. By May 2019, SunTrust had funded roughly $13 million for teammates who completed the Eight Pillars program. The result of this offering to teammates was swift and significant. Retention for new teammates who participated in the program was 77 percent, while those who did not participate had a retention rate close to 40 percent. The teller population saw the most significant impact, with 64 percent 18-month retention among participants vs. 19 percent of those who were not.

With such encouraging results, Bill Rogers wanted to explore the opportunity to offer the program for corporate clients through wholesale operations. However, the team initially designed the business case as a non-profit enterprise. "There are a lot of companies that offer financial education services only as a trojan horse into client organizations to cross-sell them into more products. We were not going to do that," recalled Bill. The team created a product that the bank could manage as an unbranded social enterprise, run at cost, and offer to other companies. This product would serve as a way for other CEOs to increase the financial well-being of their employees without strings attached. "When CEOs and CFOs heard our proposal, they were shocked to learn we did not want to brand it. We wanted their company and leaders to get the credit, to be the heroes," said Bill. Companies like Delta, Home Depot, Rollins, Gas South, and First Data embedded the program into their employee benefit systems, and the work started to deepen their relationship with SunTrust.

Despite the progress, Bill and his team still faced an uphill battle selling the social impact initiative internally because bankers were used to valuing quarterly results rather than initiatives that paid off in the long term. The challenge was particularly difficult with the wholesale bank business, but the financial fitness program and its impact on the relationship with corporate clients helped change the dynamic. By 2019 200 companies were customizing the product to create their own financial well-being programs for their employees, which became another tangible contribution to the bank's purpose.

Expanding the Footprint

The bank launched a revamped intranet page to host in-house webinars and team sessions that built momentum for the social impact work throughout the firm. It soon became evident that many teammates were excited and inspired by the bank's purpose. The leadership team realized that teammates who felt passionate about SunTrust's social impact would want to help integrate it at different levels. As a result, the SunTrust team created the Purpose Ambassador (PA) program. PAs became a major channel for expanding the footprint of the bank's purpose internally and externally.

The PA group was comprised of high-performing teammates who applied to serve as ambassadors for SunTrust's social impact in addition to their regular work responsibilities. They would be specially trained in articulating and encouraging the social impact message. With almost 100 at the launch, applications came in at higher-than-expected rates and were finally capped at 500 for the inaugural cohort. The group selected 50 leaders who were each assigned about 20 purpose ambassadors. These leaders hosted local get-togethers with other PAs in order to stay geographically and physically connected.

The program empowered PAs to shape their roles in ways they found relevant to their area of work, but at the core, they existed to help make purpose real in their organization. Each leader received special training and tools to facilitate their responsibilities, such as the creation of conversation cards that suggested ideas on how to incorporate the bank's social impact purpose into client engagement. The cards encouraged teammates to offer their personal journeys towards financial well-being and ask questions to understand the client in a more personal way. They included suggestions such as "Talk about what matters most to you," "Who has helped you the most?" or "Who would you most like to help and why?" The PA training also included a workshop created in partnership with a company that specialized in personalizing purpose.

The PA playbook provided guidelines for how teammates could make the social impact relevant to their work, along with monthly programs to encourage more engagement. The challenges were aligned with business goals and helped the ambassadors keep the purpose conversation connected to the business conversation. If the two were to separate, it could become a problem. In fact, Bill emphasized this point by saying, "Our purpose represents the business that we are in. It is how we compete. It is not a charity program, or something done on the side." The purpose ambassadors also became critical to collecting feedback about opportunities for improvement. For instance, it was a PA who noticed the challenge that many parents face when talking about financial security with their kids. The team eventually partnered with a children's book author to create a series of tools that could help parents engage with their children on issues of financial well-being. In a separate instance, a purpose ambassador experienced the challenge of helping her elderly parents with their financial stability. She quickly saw that as another opportunity for the bank to light the way to financial well-being. Her input resulted in the creation of a boot camp program to help adults with elderly parents learn to support their financial decisions in the later stages of life.

The new organizational structure that Bill spearheaded early in his tenure made the integration of their social impact efforts more organic by incorporating it into management routines. For instance, performance review conversations started to integrate purpose-related considerations. Teammates who demonstrated ways of embedding social impact in their day-to-day work were celebrated. As the message continued to evolve, managers kept purpose at the forefront by challenging teammates and asking them how they were embedding social impact into their work routines.

To help teammates integrate the purpose initiative in their personal lives, SunTrust introduced a "Day of Purpose"—a full day off each year for all teammates to focus on their personal financial well-being. It became commonplace to ask teammates if they had taken their Day of Purpose or recommend them to do so. Management encouraged leaders to share their purpose stories with their teams to spark further conversations. For example, the Vice President of market activation and engagement conducted personal sessions with her team, openly discussing financial gaps in her family's life and how she could close those gaps with the tools provided by the purpose work. These conversations became part of routine events like Purpose Days and award ceremonies, where living purpose was celebrated and publicized. Another approach Bill often used was beginning meetings with a few minutes to share "purpose moments," which gave teammates a forum to exchange both experiences and challenges in applying the social impact goals. These conversations helped leaders identify the groundswell of change that was taking place. For instance, the foreclosure unit started to count the number of homes saved instead of the number of homes foreclosed. Every time a home was saved, teammates rang a bell, and everyone on the floor stopped their work to celebrate the fact that one more family was able to keep their home.

In addition, there were visible moments when leaders made different decisions after adopting a social impact lens. A critical moment happened in June 2018 when SunTrust faced a large-scale data breach. The initial discussion centered on how to contain the news and avoid a public relations scandal. However, during the meeting, Bill kept looking at the purpose flag hanging on the wall. "I was listening to the conversation but thinking, this is not consistent with our purpose. If we believe that being client-first is one of our values, if we believe we are lighting the way to financial well-being, then we are not leaving this meeting today without figuring out how to do a full disclosure of what happened and how to offer them the protection they need."

By the end of the meeting, they crafted a plan to announce the breach to individual clients and the public, as well as to extend identity theft protection to all bank customers, including those unaffected. "I knew that by making those decisions, I was putting many teammates in a very difficult position with their clients. However, their reaction was over the top," remembered Bill. Teammates expressed a deep sense of pride for the direction taken, and in fact, it helped facilitate the conversation with clients because it became proof of the type of purpose-driven company the bank was becoming. Guided by the purpose of work, changes in business practices, and individual behaviors were slowly transforming the operations of the bank in tangible ways.

Making Purpose Public

By the summer of 2015, the shift in company culture, driven by the purpose initiative, was palpable, and the conversation shifted toward the idea of communicating their social impact work externally. The motivation was simple: How could SunTrust aspire to light the way to financial well-being without involving the community at large? There was no disagreement on the social problems which included issues such as student loan burden, credit card debt, and foreclosures. There was no question about the social impact of personal finances. The challenge was: what was SunTrust willing to do about it?

However, going public with the purpose of work raised several concerns. For instance, how could SunTrust communicate externally in a way that could make a real difference? Should SunTrust connect its external communication about the purpose of work to the bank products and services, and if so, how? Should the bank communicate using traditional mass communication methods or in a more targeted manner? To what end and with what message? These were all questions that the chief marketing officer at SunTrust was trying to answer. She came to the bank partly inspired by the way in which purpose shaped the bank's view on growth. However, leading the strategy for taking the purpose public also meant managing uncharted and sometimes risky territory. For instance, companies like Gillette and Nike have faced criticism and even backlash when communicating their social impact initiatives to mass audiences. She recalled: "We didn't have a way of talking externally about our purpose. We didn't have the right words. 'Lighting the way to financial wellbeing' is a mouthful, and customers don't really know what it means to them." Before going external, the team at SunTrust needed to understand financial well-being from a broader perspective, not only through the lens of bank services. To do so, they embarked on an extensive research effort, conducting over 100 qualitative interviews and surveying thousands of customers to understand what "lighting the way to financial well-being" really meant. All the work yielded one critical insight: There is a difference between financial literacy, financial status, and financial stress. Financial status and financial literacy are factors that correlate with income level, but financial stress does not. The team found multiple examples of wealthy individuals experiencing levels of financial stress similar to those who were living from paycheck to paycheck. Financial stress was a root cause of many of the negative conditions these families were trying to resolve, including family disruption and adverse health effects. The antidote to financial stress was confidence. "Financial confidence is when you experience tangible control of your money," explained the CMO. "It doesn't mean you have enough money, but when you know what's coming in and what's going out, you can plan, and you get financial confidence. In our surveys, we see that it is correlated to happiness and life satisfaction. Finally, our most important finding is that anybody can achieve it."

The research gave the SunTrust team clarity on how to communicate their purpose in the market and enabled them to focus on a social impact benefit they could realistically achieve. It also helped inform a more relevant way of describing the problem to people than speaking about "lighting the way to financial well-being." As the problem and external messaging became clear, the team still needed a strategy for how to lead the change. Companies the size of SunTrust traditionally invest in CSR advertising to generate awareness about their good deeds in the market. However, that approach would not help their goal of elevating the financial confidence of people in the community. They started to consider a more proactive path, believing that if SunTrust were indeed a purpose-driven bank and anyone could achieve financial confidence, they may need to organize a movement rather than just a message. As a result, many senior leaders united around the idea of championing a movement for financial confidence. Like other movements, they needed a mission and a name. They called it "Momentum onUp," and their societal mission achieved a new level of clarity—to help five million people take steps toward financial confidence.

The number was ambitious, and measurement became a key challenge. As Bill recalls: "People got nervous at the beginning and posed a lot of difficult questions. For instance, how tightly do we have to audit it? We needed to have high integrity in the measuring of things we're doing, but it doesn't need to have the level of an audit because we're not saying it in a financial statement. So, I just said we are going for five million, and you know what, we'll figure it out. And we did. We created a dashboard that counted the number of people taking our financial confidence training every day. It was really motivating for teammates to see the number of people we were helping, and no matter where you are in the company, you know that the work you are doing is important."

When the team decided to launch a movement and commit to a tangible goal, they did not know what the implications would be, so they assigned a group to figure it out. One of its leaders explained it this way, "we kept going back to our purpose, which is *lighting the way*. If we are really serious about this, then we have to launch a movement for everybody, and if we are going to launch a movement, then we need to take a stand. The leadership team spent many days trying to determine what stand they were going to take and debated every word before deciding on one statement—*everybody can achieve financial confidence to live a life well spent*."

To launch a movement, SunTrust needed to invest in a wide-reaching message. For the first time, the team bought a commercial spot during the Super Bowl. This became SunTrust's most expensive campaign. The advertisement does not reference the bank, its services, or its locations except for its logo at the end; the bulk of the time is spent launching the movement for financial confidence. The Super Bowl ad helped announce the external movement to SunTrust's internal teammates and inspire their participation. In fact, management set a goal of getting 100 percent employee participation in the movement before going public. The effort culminated in an event called "On Live." Bill Rogers and the executive team went on a three-city tour to places where SunTrust had the largest concentration of teammates. The leadership team traveled to Richmond, Orlando, and Atlanta, all cities with large business operations. They rented out convention centers and concert halls and created events where thousands of teammates participated in the unveiling of the work. Bill explained, "We shared with our teammates what was going to make us different moving forward. We showed them our Super Bowl ad to launch the onUp movement. It was unlike us to do something like that, but we did, and we touched...15,000 of our 25,000 teammates' lives." Consequently, the team saw significant improvement in employee engagement scores, in particular, a 5.8 percent increase in how proud teammates felt to work at SunTrust. Also, it was the only quarter in over six years in which brand awareness and consideration grew among potential customers.

At first, the SunTrust team was divided on how, or even if, to commercialize the purpose-based product. Bill himself was apprehensive about investing in a Super Bowl commercial with so little connection to the brand. Ultimately, the team felt that it was important to keep the onUp Movement separate from the commercial side of the business and instead drive a culture change that would organically grow the business by building trust. The same applied to communication across digital channels and the website. There was no link between the OnUp movement and SunTrust services. However, while the decision not to brand SunTrust's purpose-related projects helped build trust and grow the business, some at the leadership level felt that after a year of building trust, it was time to brand the purpose products and connect them to the commercial side. Some thought the bank had done too good of a job keeping SunTrust separate from the onUp movement, to the extent that now there was little awareness among customers about their role in the program. For example, participants who discovered via onUp that they could save by refinancing could not easily navigate to SunTrust's mortgage product. Therefore, keeping the social impact purpose disconnected from the SunTrust brand created a public movement that made an impact inside and outside the organization, some leaders thought the next iteration of the movement should include careful connections to SunTrust products. However, it was not clear how to do that without impacting the authenticity and credibility behind the OnUp program.

A final consideration for making the purpose public involves measuring the effectiveness of the initiative. It was one thing to measure the number of people participating in the programs, but a more important measure was to assess how financial confidence was changing among participants. There was no clear metric of financial confidence, so the team needed to create one. Starting in March 2016,[1] SunTrust commissioned ongoing nationwide polling from an independent firm, MaritzCX. The survey asked individuals to assess themselves based on their actions pertaining to five core behaviors of financial confidence: budgeting, debt management, savings, maximizing income, and retirement planning. For example, respondents were asked to rate themselves on statements such as, "I have a budget I stick to every month" and "I am making progress saving for retirement." The firm working with the SunTrust team created the Financial Confidence Index which focused on the consumer's mastery of his or her own financial behavior. SunTrust managing director and chief market strategist reflected on its impact by saying, "While the economy is growing and indicators show that Americans are optimistic, the Financial Confidence Index illustrates that many people are still not taking control and developing strong habits around money." He added, "Across all income levels, our research shows a correlation among Americans that cite high financial confidence and report behaviors to actively manage their money—such as using a budget, managing debt, saving regularly, maximizing their income and planning for retirement. Those with positive money habits also report greater life satisfaction."

By the time the merger with BB&T was announced in 2019, SunTrust was seven years into a journey toward embedding a purpose with social impact into the company. From 2011 through 2018, SunTrust's financial metrics improved each year with the long-term Total Shareholder Return (TSR) of 214 percent, first among its eleven peer banks and well above the peer bank's TSR median of 166 percent. Reflecting on SunTrust's path, Bill felt good about the work they had accomplished. "Purpose is a bit like innovation. Anybody can innovate. Innovation is easy. The hard part is to scale it. Doing purpose at scale is very hard."

Bill knew that the focus on social impact and purpose had become a core enabler of much of the success at SunTrust. It facilitated the creation of a customer-centric culture and changed behavior among teammates. It drove higher levels of collaboration needed to serve customers in new and better ways, and it rekindled the pride of many wearing the SunTrust badge. Still, there was much more he thought they could do to live up to the potential of a purpose-driven company. "I know we have accomplished a lot, but I feel like we are just rounding first base, simply getting started," Bill remarked.

As illustrated by this case, competing on social impact can become a way of aligning and uplifting the organization, let alone helping it find growth. But to be successful, it is critical for leaders to not only support but also embrace the integration of social impact into the growth strategies of the firm. SunTrust's approach demonstrates the importance of integrating a social impact purpose with core business strategies rather than treating it as a separate philanthropic or CSR initiative. The bank's purpose, "Lighting the Way to Financial Wellbeing," was not just a slogan, but a guiding principle that influenced business decisions and operations. The footprint of social impact at Suntrust was also broad, impacting the formation of new structures like the dedicated channels and roles to ensure the bank embedded the work across various facets of the organization, including human resources, product development, corporate partnerships, and community engagement. This alignment helped ensure that their social impact mission was reflected in everyday actions and decision-making processes. The case also underscores that embedding social impact requires a long-term commitment and should be seen as a strategic enabler rather than a short-term marketing campaign. This approach helped SunTrust achieve significant improvements in employee engagement, brand perception, and financial performance over time.

SunTrust's success in building trust both internally and externally was rooted in its authentic approach to social impact and the leadership practices adopted by Bill Rogers and others in the firm. By addressing issues like financial stress and confidence directly, the bank was engaging employees and customers meaningfully. The internal financial wellness program for employees exemplified this authenticity and demonstrated the bank's commitment to its purpose. The decision to ensure internal buy-in and practice the purpose initiatives internally before communicating them externally helped maintain credibility. SunTrust's decision to create a societal movement for financial confidence rather than merely a marketing campaign was pivotal. The "Momentum onUp" movement aimed to make a broader social impact by helping millions achieve financial confidence, thus aligning the bank's purpose with a tangible societal benefit. Finally, SunTrust developed the Financial Confidence Index to measure the effectiveness of its initiatives. By quantifying the effect on behavioral changes and financial confidence, the bank was able to assess its impact on both employees and the broader community, thereby reinforcing its commitment and credibility in the market.

Note

1   www.prnewswire.com/news-releases/suntrust-introduces-financial-confidence-index-300627111.html.

Chapter 14

The Future of "Good Growth"

When managers consider their market environment, the focus tends to be on economic, technological, or competitive conditions. If consumer confidence is healthy or technology improves to enable more efficient operations it creates a more conducive path to growth. However, managers seeking to grow brands and businesses in the 21st century will have to account in new ways for the well-being of our communities and the state of our planet. According to the 2023 progress report by the United Nations on the Sustainable Development Goals, the world is far off track in achieving the targets agreed upon a decade ago. Back in 2012, the ambition was to eliminate poverty and hunger, promote healthier societies, empower women and girls, and confront the environmental crises emerging from climate change, pollution, and the degradation of biodiversity. The report summarizes our current condition in one word – stagnation. In fact, in some goals, we are collectively slipping backward and moving further away from the targets, particularly in efforts to reduce inequality, achieve food security, or prevent the extinction of species, let alone slow down the impacts of climate change.

Brand leaders in the 21st century will not have the luxury of ignoring these macro conditions. As the UN report states, climate shifts will change conditions across borders, introducing disruptions to supply chains, markets, and the availability of natural resources. Limited access to water, food, education, and opportunity will continue to fuel mass migrations and ignite conflict and instability across markets. These trends impose a risk to the sustainability or even viability of some businesses. They will also change consumer expectations towards institutions, governments, and companies. The private sector is a critical actor in the pursuit of prosperity in the world and in our collective ability to enhance the well-being of more people. With the ways brands see markets and customer needs, design and sell products or services, and eventually repurpose them – they can make a significant contribution toward both their investors and their communities. Competing on social impact requires the capability to do both, identifying societal needs well suited for a brand, and understanding the methods and decisions involved in creating societal benefits that can make an offering more attractive, leading to good growth.

DOI: 10.4324/9781003383246-15

The 2024 Spring CMO survey from Duke University points out challenges facing marketing executives attempting to address societal challenges. First is resources, given that marketing budgets on sustainability-related issues are approximately 1.9 percent of their funds and are projected to grow to 4.5 percent in five years. Also, nearly a third of the firms surveyed appear to be taking no social impact action. Limited resources and lack of motivation are part of the challenges that aspiring social impact leaders will face. Yet, the main difficulty confronting managers is the heightened politicization of economic activity. Brand and firm actions have become a new source of content for political activists across both sides of the spectrum to raise awareness of their causes or provoke disruptions in the system in ways that benefit their movements or reap economic gains from their followers. The active threats, boycotts, and criticisms that Target received by placing merchandise friendly to transgender customers or the rejection by some customers of Coca-Cola's Arctic Home program due to its association with climate change are not trivial concerns for managers who want to pursue good growth. No one wants to be on the receiving end of those responses, and the likelihood of their occurrence is only going to grow as communication technology makes it easier for individual voices to reach mainstream audiences. However, seeking growth is always risky. Innovation is risky. New products are risky. New markets are risky. Failure and criticism are and always have been a part of any form of competition and many individual endeavors. That in itself should not stop progress if there is reason to believe that social impact strategies offer a path to a new type of growth better suited to the needs and realities of today. The fact is, the evidence is overwhelming in the direction of social impact. We began this book by sharing dozens of examples of how companies, large and small, new and old, were integrating societal benefits into their products and services. Importantly, it also shows how their creation of societal benefits enabled them to disrupt markets and unlock good growth, like in the case of Brita, Chipotle, or Dove. Brands like Allbirds are showing how lower carbon emissions can become a new product feature. Blueland, Boxed Water and HP are designing waste out of their product lifecycle, giving customers a reason to remain loyal. Creating more inclusive environments is helping brands like Sephora or Barbie accelerate their performance and become hard to catch. Keeping with this upbeat tone, the 2024 Spring CMO survey points to more than 50 percent of firms planning to launch new products with sustainability benefits embedded in their offerings, with a focus on addressing climate change challenges. We believe this will create good growth for firms.

Greater optimism emerges from our research examining the public signing of the Business Roundtable (BRT) Purpose of a Corporation Statement, which promises to deliver value for customers, employees, suppliers, and society, in addition to shareholders. The nearly 200 firms that signed this shift in purpose included JPMorganChase, Amazon, Apple, and Bank of

America. While some viewed the BRT statement signing as a call for governance and capitalism reform, reactions to the announcement were both swift and mixed, with over 325 news reports during the first week after the news release came out. Many Op-Ed writers argued against it, with critics viewing it as purpose-washing, a distraction, and a mistake. We conducted a systematic assessment. Treating the signing as an experiment allowed us to apply an econometric approach often used in developmental economics. We matched the firms that signed the pledge with firms that did not on a number of firm and industry representation characteristics. Effectively, the two groups were not different from each other in terms of size, profits, industry representation, etc. The only difference was whether or not they signed the declaration. Our analysis showed that firms that shifted from investor primacy or investor-alone focus to stakeholders (focus on customers, society, employees, suppliers, and investors), increased customer satisfaction and employee engagement two to three years after the signing year relative to the matched sample of non-signatory firms. While the corporate purpose shift lowered the financial strength of the signatories for two years, the effect did not last. Overall, we show that corporate purpose focused on multiple stakeholders rather than just shareholders is achievable and beneficial to most stakeholders, if not all, in the long run.

There is a difference between good growth and bad growth. The 20th century was filled with innovation, economic development, and, at times, prosperity in many countries. But the forms and methods of business imposed too high a cost on our environment and society. Finding growth is essential to economic and human development, but the type of growth matters. Good growth is balanced, mindful, conscious, and innovative. We hope this book helps create more of it.

Index

For Product Safety Concerns and Information please contact our EU
representative GPSR@taylorandfrancis.com
Taylor & Francis Verlag GmbH, Kaufingerstraße 24, 80331 München, Germany

www.ingramcontent.com/pod-product-compliance
Lightning Source LLC
Chambersburg PA
CBHW061253220326
41599CB00028B/5639